POETRY OF THE HOLOCAUST

POETRY OF THE HOLOCAUST

an anthology

Edited and introduced by
Jean Boase-Beier
and
Marian de Vooght

Arc
PUBLICATIONS
2019

Published by Arc Publications
Nanholme Mill, Shaw Wood Road
Todmorden, OL14 6DA, UK
www.arcpublications.co.uk

Design by Tony Ward
Printed in Great Britain by T.J. International Ltd,
Padstow, Cornwall

978 1911469 05 6 (pbk)

Cover photograph:
Railway track into Buchenwald
by Jean Boase-Beier

Arc Publications gratefully acknowledges the support of
the Dutch Foundation for Literature (letterenfonds.nl) and
Flanders Literature (flandersliterature.be).

FLANDERS LITERATURE

Nederlands
letterenfonds
dutch foundation
for literature

Supported using public funding by
**ARTS COUNCIL
ENGLAND**
LOTTERY FUNDED

**Arc Publications
Anthologies in Translation
Series Editor: Jean Boase-Beier**

CONTENTS

Introduction / 15

ACKNOWLEDGEMENTS

The Publishers and Editors would like to thank all poets and families of poets and translators and other copyright-holders who have given us permission to include poems and translations in this volume. A detailed list of copyright-holders / publishers is given at the end of the volume. For some of the poems, we have been unable to find copyright-holders, but would be grateful for any contact details.

We would like to thank all translators of the poems in this Anthology; their names are given after each poem they have translated, and more information on them is given at the back of the book. We would also like to thank everyone who has done earlier versions of poems we have translated ourselves. We have tried to read these wherever possible, and they are sure to have influenced us.

In addition, we would particularly like to thank the following people for their help in locating poems, for commenting on translation problems and drafts, providing transliterations, and discussing the project with us: Raficq Abdulla; Nozomi Abe; Dror Abend-David; Jeremy Adler; Lela Banakas; Sidonia Bauer; Dieter Beier; Marianne Bertsch-Junger; Daina Chiba; Han Dorussen; John Fletcher; Hazel Frankel; Iain Galbraith; Atar Hadari; Bill Jackson; Wanda Józwikowska; Eva Laantee Reintamm; Ilmar Lehtpere; Fanny Loreaud; Ton Naaijkens; Paschalis Nikolaou; Robert Parzer; Sonja Rethy; Anthony Rudolf; Fiona Sampson; Lizzy Robinson-Self; George Szirtes.

INTRODUCTION

What is the purpose of an anthology of translated Holocaust poetry? There are many ways of answering this question. To give voice to victims we may not have heard of. To show that there is more to Holocaust poetry than we suspected. To show what happens when we translate such poetry.

These are some of the reasons, but there are many others. The anthology arose out of a research project 'Translating the Poetry of the Holocaust', funded by the Arts and Humanities Research Council, that we carried out at the University of East Anglia in 2013-14. We wanted to find out who had written poetry during, or about, the Holocaust, why they had done so, what languages they had written in, and how much Holocaust poetry had been translated. We also wanted to know more about the importance of such poetry, for its writers and for its readers. And we wanted to consider specific problems of its translation.

Holocaust poetry has at least two main characteristics that make it unique. It was written as a result of the events of the Holocaust, because poets needed to respond poetically to what was happening, or had happened, or even, on occasion, what they feared was about to happen. The second defining characteristic is that it is a response written in poetry. It is important to understand exactly what this means.

Holocaust poetry is like other poetry in that it uses poetic figures – the shape of lines on the page, repeated patterns of sound, ambiguous expressions that cannot be resolved one way or the other – to engage and hold the reader's attention. But it differs from other poetry in the way such figures are used. Rhymes and a regular rhythm can suggest lightness but they have the opposite effect in a poem about hatred of the Jews (Alfred Kerr's 'The Most Afflicted' p. 36).

Repeated sounds in Felix Swoboda's 'Storm' (p. 31) suggest both fear and inertia, and the powerlessness we feel when we wait for what must come. Ambiguity, in Holocaust poems, might be a gap in the text, as at the end of Gertrud Kolmar's 'The Abused' (p. 94). The reader has to mentally insert something – but what?

Like all poetry, Holocaust poetry uses poetic means to create an impression, convey feeling, or to create such feeling in its readers. But it is responding to catastrophic and specific events. Thus it tends not to generalise, but to particularize: the man in his prison cell in Dietrich Bonhoeffer's 'Who am I?' (p. 90), the sight of old people arriving on a new transport at Terezín in H. G. Adler's 'Arrival of the Old People' (p. 49), the murder of the poet's newborn baby in the Vilnius ghetto in Abraham Sutzkever's 'To the Child' (p. 51).

In these poems, the individual voice is everything. And this is why we wanted to do something a little different from other anthologies of Holocaust poetry (such as Hilda Schiff's 1995 anthology *Holocaust Poetry*), many of which provided us with initial inspiration and the impetus to research further. We wanted to give readers access to a wider range of individual voices: to the wheelchair-bound Polish resistance fighter whose wheelchair was removed by the Gestapo when she was imprisoned (Irena Bobowska's 'So I learn life's greatest art...' p. 87), to the anonymous writer in the Auschwitz 'Zigeunerlager', the 'Gypsy Camp', ('Song of the Roma' p. 56), to the poet with Down's writing today, responding to what happened during the Holocaust to others with Down's Syndrome (Angela Fritzen's 'The urns...' p. 224).

We also wanted to show that a very wide range of languages was involved. So we have collected Japanese tanka written by Yukiko Sugihara in Lithuania where her husband, the Japanese consul, helped the persecuted escape via Japan (p. 100), poetry by the Norwegian writer whose Jewish lover was transported to Auschwitz (Gunvor Hofmo's 'Encounter' p. 121), by the young German-speaking Czernowitz poet, Selma Meerbaum-Eisinger, who was never able to fulfil her ambitions ('Tragedy' p. 28). The Nazis wanted to annihilate everyone who was different and silence every voice of protest. These are the people we want to celebrate.

One might wonder why people composed poetry in such extreme circumstances – in prisons, in camps, in hiding, with bound hands, on scraps of paper, in their heads. But poetry does what documentary accounts can struggle to do. It makes the reader feel, it triggers a sense of recognition, of injustice, of anger. It was one of the very few ways for those in captivity to experience brief moments of freedom and control. Knowing that the Nazis intended whole peoples to die, and their languages, such as Yiddish or Ladino or Romani, to die with them, there must have been a necessary and sustaining sense of resistance in writing in these languages. Knowing that the Nazis wanted poetry and art to be enslaved to the Nazi cause, writing about their experiences of victimhood in the ways they chose to write was an act of defiance.

Sometimes the poet was writing specifically to communicate with those who would come later: poems composed in the ghettos in Warsaw and other (mainly Polish) cities were part of the Jewish tradition of responding to tragedy with poetry. Poems were carefully hidden, or smuggled out, in the hope that they, at least, would survive. Sometimes the poetry arose from a need to make sense of events, perhaps even an attempt to explain to oneself what could not be explained. But there was always an imagined reader, because poetry – especially poetry written under such circumstances, or later, as a response to them – is communication. For this reason it is important not to take out of context Adorno's much-quoted worry that poetry after Auschwitz was barbaric. Of course, Adorno was right to reject the aestheticizing of the Holocaust. But poems (and other forms of art) as necessary communication do not aestheticize.

It is because poetry communicates that it requires and invites translation. Translation – especially of such work – is never about getting it right, about approximating the form or content of the original, about making a rough copy for those who do not speak Yiddish, or Latvian or French. It is about recognising someone else's story, understanding the way the teller has chosen to tell it, and passing it on to others. Of course, to do this it is necessary to know the original language. But, more than this, you have to discover what the poet was doing with the original language: how it was transformed, how it was shaped, how it was made to fit or to undermine its content.

For this reason, we have not only spent several years researching the Holocaust and its poetry, but, for this anthology, we have recruited a large number of translators, advisers, checkers and informants. Reading Holocaust poetry in translation, we feel, should not just be an aid to learning about the Holocaust. It should be about hearing the stories of those who cannot (or can no longer) speak for themselves, in the voices of others who do their best to speak for them. From the translator's point of view, every time we tell someone else's story we add to it: translating a poem underlines its function as communication, and helps it to live on in a new context.

Some of the challenges the translators have faced have to do with the difficulties of grasping events at historical and geographical distance, and, as with any translation, the problems of rendering the sounds and structures of German or Polish or Russian in English. Most of all there is a need for the skill that only poetry translators have, of recognising the specific link between the poet's story and the way the original language is used, and capturing that link in a new language.

The anthology contains poems both by victims of the Holocaust and by those who take their part. This means that all the poems collected here are written from the heart, and each poem was chosen because it gives us the opportunity to think about how people were affected by the events they witnessed or are reflecting on.

Because the Nazis persecuted people they perceived as 'other', setting up programmes to remove unwanted groups from society, it was important to us not to arrange the poems in this anthology, written by and about people from many different backgrounds, according to those backgrounds or to the languages in which they wrote. No group of people is ever homogeneous and people who share the same background – religious, linguistic, political or otherwise – do not necessarily experience events the same way. Any group can harbour protesters, victims, bystanders, and persecutors, and in some cases a person's position is ambiguous. The fact that von Törne was the son of a Nazi complicates his perspective but does not make him a perpetrator. The well-known and often translated Hungarian poet János Pilinszky clearly felt great empathy for the suffering of victims, but in fact he witnessed the horror of the camps as an officer in the Hungarian army.

If we had arranged the poems according to the persecuted group the poet or subject of the poem belongs to we might seem on the one hand to be labelling people ('The Jews', 'Communists', 'The Disabled', 'Homosexuals') and would on the other hand be failing to acknowledge their ambiguities, as well as the uniqueness of each poem as a reaction to the Holocaust. Nor would a division on the basis of language do justice to the identity of individual poets. Many poets are bi- or multilingual and many would identify with more than one culture or none at all. Poets have written poems in Yiddish in such diverse places as Lithuania, South Africa, Israel and Poland. Or, to take another example, poet Iboja Wandall-Holm was originally from Czechoslovakia but ended up writing in Danish after she had survived several concentration camps and found a new life in Denmark. Edith Bruck was born in Hungary, then adopted Italy as her country and Italian as a new language after her survival. Jewish poets in Greece, Turkey and parts of former Yugoslavia wrote in Ladino, and non-Jewish poets have responded in Greek to the fate of their Sephardic neighbours. Each poem shows connectedness to the suffering in a unique way – by experience, memory, empathy and just by the effort of thinking about what it means to be a victim of the Holocaust.

The poems are grouped into three sections according to the perspective they take, rather than solely by the date of writing. Those in Section I, the shortest section, reveal fear and despair at the signs that something terrible was coming, and this anthology is the only one so far to contain poems from well before the start of the Second World War. The oldest poem in the collection is Eduard Saenger's 'Premonition' (p. 28), which dates from 1932. The presentiments people had in the 1930s were brought about by concrete and visible discrimination against Jews and other groups of people in Germany even before the Nazis came to power in 1933. Imprisonment of political dissenters started in 1933, and the first concentration camp – Dachau – was established. Jews were encouraged to emigrate; occasional, random killings happened from the start of the regime. In 1933 there were also the Nazi book burnings in Berlin, in 1937 the *Entartete Kunst* (Degenerate Art) exhibition of modern art in Munich, in 1938 the vandalizing of Jewish shops, synagogues and houses during *Kristallnacht* (Night of Broken Glass). That same year saw the start of the systematic removal of citizenship from Jewish Germans, and the following year the start of the Euthanasia programme with the aim of killing people with disabilities. Poems written in reaction to events like these, and included in Section I, are, for example, those by Dutch poets Jan Campert and Ed. Hoornik, who, though not Jewish themselves, wrote poems of outrage and alarm about the burning of the books and pogroms that were happening across the border.

Section II contains poems that show the horror of persecution in the form of forced labour, confinement in ghettos, imprisonment, deportation to camps, abuse, starvation and murder. Many poems tell of the extreme circumstances of being hollowed-out by hunger, disease and abuse in concentration camps. Some poems were literally written on the verge of collapse, such as Miklós Radnóti's 'Postcard (4)' (p. 96), or imagine the final moments of victims (Nelly Sachs' 'They no longer weep and wail...' p. 80). Others, like those of Adler or Sutzkever, describe life in ghettos or camps, or, like the poems of Kolmar or Bonhoeffer, take the perspective of those imprisoned for their political or religious views. In Bonhoeffer's case, as in that of Alfred Schmidt-Sas ('Strange Lightness of Life so Close to Death' p. 92) the poets were writing in the knowledge that they were about to be executed.

The poems in Section III tell of the lasting trauma of the Holocaust, as recorded by survivors, family members and other poets. The time after the Holocaust is still ongoing and Holocaust poetry will continue to be written not only as long as there are survivors, but as long as there are poets who think about the victims with empathy. Poetry by survivors reflects the ways they carry the experience of the Holocaust with them. For some it is how they identify themselves, as in Ceija Stojka's 'auschwitz is my overcoat' (p. 152). For others it is something hidden, internal, but also always there, as when, in Saul van Messel's poem, the wind blows open the metaphorical coat of the poet's words, to reveal the 'lining / of my thought' (p. 200). This final section is the longest, and has poems from 1946 onwards. The most recent poems in the anthology, such as Stanislav Smelyansky's 'Guilty!' (p. 209), are just a few years old.

The history of the writing of Holocaust poetry is bound up with translation. This is true for many of those whose work appears in English translation here, and it also applies to many English-language poets who wrote about the Holocaust. Thus, the English-language poet and translator Michael Hamburger was born in Berlin but emigrated with his parents to the United Kingdom in 1933. Karen Gershon first wrote poetry in German but, after coming to the UK on the Kindertransport in 1938, she wrote in English. Anthony Hecht, who was born in New York to German-Jewish parents, served in the division of the US Army that liberated Flossenbürg concentration camp, where he interviewed prisoners in French – an experience that had a lasting effect on his poetry. Irish poet and linguist Michael O'Siadhail's poems in reaction to the events of the Holocaust, collected in *The Gossamer Wall* (2002), are steeped in years of listening to and reading survivor accounts and include quotations from other poets in their original languages and in English translation.

The work of English-language Holocaust poets is already accessible to English speakers and so this anthology contains only non-English poems, translated from around twenty languages. The original poems are also included, so that readers will feel encouraged to read or at least look at them, and note differences between the originals and the translations. Some source languages will be inaccessible to some readers, but many words in other languages can be recognised, especially in languages that share common origins with English, such as Dutch or German or Yiddish (given here in Latin script, in its varying transcriptions from the Hebrew script).

Many previously published anthologies – in various languages – are either based around the cultural background of the poets or on the concentration camp they were imprisoned in. The oldest collection is André Verdet's *Poèmes de Buchenwald* of 1946 (reissued in 1995), with poems written in or translated into French. A 2012 book edited by Wulf Kristen and Annette Seeman presents the poems from Verdet's anthology in German translation (*Der gefesselte Wald*, The Chained Forest). *I Never Saw Another Butterfly* is a book of Jewish children's poems and drawings from the Terezín concentration camp, edited by Hana Volavková (1964) and expanded by the United States Holocaust Memorial Museum (1993). Jack Lévy edited *And the World Stood Silent* (1989; 2000), a volume of Sephardic Holocaust poetry with English translations. Dorothea Heiser and Stuart Taberner's multilingual collection *My Shadow in Dachau*, containing poems by victims and survivors of that concentration camp, was published in 2014; the book first appeared as a German edition in 1993.

In the twenty-five years since the first edition of Schiff's anthology many more poems have emerged that were written by Holocaust survivors whose background was not Jewish. For example, we have included poems by Sinti poet Philomena Franz (p. 220) and Roma poet Ceija Stojka (p. 152), André Sarcq's 'To the Twice-Murdered Men (The Rag)' (p. 123), that bears witness to the persecution of gay men, and Barbara Lipinska-Leidinger's poems in response to the sites of the Euthanasia programme (pp. 140, 160, 164 and 171). The majority of these poems have never been published in English translation before. In several cases we also present new translations of work that has previously been translated.

Inevitably, readers will be able to identify gaps in the anthology. Many of these result from conscious decisions on our part. We aimed to include poems by poets less well-known in the English-speaking world and to introduce some less familiar poems by poets who do have an established name. In the case of Paul Celan, for example, we did not include his often quoted 'Death Fugue', but the poems 'Aspen tree…' (p. 112) and 'Winding Sheet' (p. 227), two relatively short poems that reveal a lasting trauma. We also did not include Yevgeny Yevtushenko's important long poem 'Babi Yar' on the shooting of 75,000 Jews in a ravine near Kiev in the autumn of 1941, because it is fairly well-known and already has a place in other anthologies. The tragedy of this massacre is thus not represented here, as it also proved difficult to trace the source texts of other poems about it, for example the 1941 eyewitness poem in Russian by Lyudmila Titova or the long Ukrainian poem written by Mykola Bazhan in 1945. Poem length in itself is a criterion on the basis of which we had to make decisions. Generally we have chosen to include shorter poems so that the voices of more poets could be heard, though we did prioritise Sarcq's very long poem, the only poem we know of that remembers gay men as victims of the Holocaust. Poems by or about Jehovah's Witnesses are lacking, on the other hand, because we could not find any, and more research is needed to establish why this is the case.

Limitations of experience and expertise on our own part and in our network of translators meant that we were unable to include poems in Romani; instead, we opted for work by Roma poets in German and Romanian and to include poems in other languages that remember Sinti and Roma victims. It is possible that we found almost no Roma and Sinti poems from the 1930s and 40s because these were oral cultures until after World War Two. The Polish-Romani poet Bronisława Wajs (whose life was portrayed in the 2016 film *Papusza*, directed by Joanna Kos-Krauze and Krisztof Krauze), was one of the very first to write in Romani after the war.

Finally, silences in the anthology can perhaps lead us to consider all those persecuted poets who could not write about their experience, for example because of the dreadful circumstances of abuse, hunger and disease in ghettos and concentration camps. Writing was also forbidden in most camps and prisons and the stories of how the poems survived are in themselves fascinating: Rivka Basman Ben-Hayim concealed poems written in Kaiserwald on scraps of paper rolled up under her tongue, René Blieck destroyed the poems he wrote in Neuengamme, but his friends memorised them. However, we must assume that many poems of the Holocaust were lost, forgotten or simply never written down.

Jean Boase-Beier & Marian de Vooght

I
AT THE BEGINNING

ROSE AUSLÄNDER

Ausländer was born in 1901 in Czernowitz, then part of Austria-Hungary, now in Ukraine. She lived in America for several years in the 1920s. From 1941 to 1944 she was forced to live in the Czernowitz ghetto. She died in Düsseldorf, in Germany, in 1988.

SNOW

Snow falls
the world turns white
In the sun
that white glitters
in every colour
White stars
blossom in the air
On the horizon
beyond the mountains
look: Snow White
and the Seven Dwarves
At night
the white is black
black as the dark queen
beyond the mountains

Translated from the German by Jean Boase-Beier

SCHNEE

Schnee fällt
die Welt wird weiß
In der Sonne
glitzert das Weiß
in allen Farben
Weiße Sterne
blühn in der Luft
Am Horizont
hinter den Bergen
sieh Schneewittchen
und die sieben Zwerge
Nachts
ist das Weiß schwarz
wie die finstere Königin
hinter den Bergen

SELMA MEERBAUM-EISINGER

The poem is dated 23 December 1941. One year later, after she had been deported, Meerbaum-Eisinger, who was Paul Celan's niece, died at the age of eighteen in the forced-labour camp Michailowka in Ukraine.

TRAGEDY

This is the worst: you pour yourself out
But no-one will know or care,
You give your whole self but have no doubt,
You'll stream like smoke in the empty air.

Translated from the German by Jean Boase-Beier

TRAGIK

Das ist das Schwerste: sich verschenken
und wissen, daß man überflüssig ist,
sich ganz zu geben und zu denken,
daß man wie Rauch ins Nichts verfließt.

EDUARD SAENGER

Born in Berlin, Saenger was a poet and translator, in particular of Shakespeare's sonnets. He fought in the First World War, and emigrated to London in 1935, where he joined the Free German League of Culture in Great Britain. He died in London in 1948. 'Vorahnung' was written in 1932.

PREMONITION

A silent wind sends fear through the land
with an edge like the howling of wolves.
How greedily the green shoots grow!
The earth trembles for its fruit
like an island about to sink.

At its limit, where the cut
of the grass mingles with the dark sweet

scent of hedge roses, where the year
breathes its deepest, enwrapped in its light
the fierce summer moves.

Translated from the German by Jean Boase-Beier

VORAHNUNG

Der leise Wind durchbangt das Land
als schwänge er Geheul von Wölfen.
Wie gierig schießen die Gewächse!
Die Erde bangt um ihre Frucht
gleich einer Insel, die versinken wird.

An seiner Grenze, wo der Schnitt
des Grases mit der dunklen Süße
der Heckenrosen duftet, wo das Jahr
am tiefsten atmet, geht verhüllt
in seinem Licht der starke Sommer.

MATILDA OLKINAITĖ

In 1941, Olkinaitė, aged nineteen, was shot by local Nazi collaborators, together with other members of the two Jewish families in the Lithuanian village Panemunėlis. In this poem from 1938, the term "Gnosiology" (philosophy of knowledge) refers to Eastern Christianity.

DURING THE GNOSIOLOGY LESSON

Beyond Three Hills
The Sun went down.
It was dusk
When we set out.

A Black Angel
Carried off the Sun.
Beyond Three Hills
The Sun has set.

Farewell, farewell –
We will never return –
We've already gone,
Beyond Three Hills.

And we did not find there
Our beloved Sun.
We only found
The dark night –

Beyond Three Hills
The Sun has set.
Oh, farewell, farewell.
We will never return.

And flowers will bloom
In the early morning –
In the early morning,
We will never return.

Translated from the Lithuanian by Laima Vincė

PER GNOSEOLOGIJOS PAMOKĄ

Už trijų kalnų
Saulė leidosi…
Vėlų vakarą
Mes išėjome

Juodas Angelas
Saulę nunešė –
Už trijų kalnų
Saulė leidosi.

Ak, sudie, sudie,
Nebegrįšime –
Jau atėjome
Už trijų kalnų –

Ir neradom ten
Saulės mylimos.
O atradom tik
Tamsų vakarą –

Už trijų kalnų
Saulė leidosi –
Ak, sudie, sudie –
Mes negrįšime.

Daug gėlių žydės
Ankstų rytmetį –
Ankstų rytmetį
Nebegrįšime.

WILHELM FELIX SWOBODA

This poem was written in 1939. Swoboda, born in 1914, was a German literary critic and musician who was active in student resistance to the Nazis at Munich University. He was sent to the Eastern front and was killed near Moscow in 1941.

STORM

Huts stilled in fear.
Giant pools. Deer.
Kneeling farmers plead
at the icon's feet.

Flame tries to die.
Clock dares not strike.
Hellish riders race
through the accursed day.

Translated from the German by Jean Boase-Beier

STURM

Angstgebannte Hütten.
Riesenlachen. Wild.
Knieende Bauern bitten
vor dem Heiligenbild.

Flamme will versagen.
Uhr wagt nicht den Schlag.
Höllische Reiter jagen
durch den verdammten Tag.

ED. HOORNIK

Hoornik notes that Grenadierstraat was a Jewish shopping district in Berlin. He wrote 'Pogrom' on 12 November 1938, two days after Kristallnacht. *His work as a journalist and poet was banned from 1942, when the Nazis took over the newspaper he worked for. He died in Amsterdam in 1970.*

POGROM

Is that the moon, whose last quarter I can see,
or a face, veiled in smoke and flame?
Where is Berlin and where Grenadier Street?
– What did the boy do, when the mob came?

Is that his shadow, standing at the river,
is this the water, that took him in,
this here the Spree, Grenadier Street over there?
– It is the Amstel, it is Amsterdam.

On Rembrandt Square, the sheen of the lamps.
Over the roofs a fountain of light shines.
– I press my nails deeper into my hands.

Jodenbree Street is a deep ravine.
Between the walls a brief scream sounds
– It's only ten hours by rail to Berlin.

Translated from the Dutch by Marian de Vooght

POGROM

Is dat de maan, die naar het laatst kwartier gaat,
of een gelaat, omspeeld door walm en vlam?
Waar is Berlijn en waar de Grenadierstraat?
– Wat deed die jongen, toen de bende kwam?

Is dat zijn schim, die daar voor de rivier staat,
is dit het water, dat hem tot zich nam,
is hier de Spree, en daar de Grenadierstraat?
– Het is de Amstel, het is Amsterdam.

Op 't Rembrandtplein gaan de lantarens branden.
Over de daken sproeit een lichtfontein.
– Ik druk mijn nagels dieper in mijn handen.

De Jodenbreestraat is een diep ravijn.
Een korte schreeuw weerkaatst tussen de wanden.
– Het is maar tien uur sporen naar Berlijn.

ALFRED KERR

Kerr, born in Breslau in 1867, was a well-known German theatre critic. He left Germany in 1933, and wrote this poem in 1933-4. He was an outspoken opponent of the Nazis, who burned his books in May 1933. He died on his first post-war visit to Germany in 1948.

WORLD IN TURMOIL...

World in turmoil… the garden of Earth
gleams with a dead suspicious light.
Horror grins. The huns set out.
The others whisper, wonder, wait –
      And then sit tight.

The German state is rotten and rank.
The toxic air is heavy and foul.
Blood rules. Earth fears
the dark ages will come again:
they whet their axes ready to strike,
the folk of the great Third Troglodyte-Reich;
and stepping in front of their "standards" and "squads"
the murderous bandit, the goblin in brown.
The others whisper, wonder, wait –
      And then sit tight.

Why? Because of the sacred creed
"don't get involved", "pay no heed".
And if the devils took over the world,
no-one would try to intervene:
we don't do that, we can't do that!
That's what they call diplomacy.
Even in cataclysmic times
"Internal affairs", they cry.

Some of them murder without a care
sanctified and above the law
The others whisper, and sit and stare.

Translated from the German by Jean Boase-Beier

VERWORRENE WELT...

Verworrene Welt ... Der Erdengarten
erglänzt in fahl-verdächtigem Licht.
Das Grauen grinst. Die Hunnen starten.
Die andren flüstern, wägen, warten –
    Und rühren sich nicht.

Deutschland verrottet und verroht.
Die Luft von Giften schwül und schwer.
Das Blutrecht herrscht. Dem Erdball droht
der dunklen Urzeit Wiederkehr;
man schärft das Beil zum großen Streich
im Dritten Troglodytenreich;
schon stelzt vor "Staffeln" und "Standarten"
der Mordbandit, der braune Wicht;
die andren flüstern, wägen, warten –
    Und rühren sich nicht.

Warum? das ist die heilige Lehre:
Strenges Verbot "sich einzumischen".
Und wenn die Welt voll Teufel wäre!
Fährt keiner dazwischen;
das tut man nie, das darf man nie!
Dies Ganze nennt sich: Diplomatie.
Es gibt in apokalyptischen Zeiten
"Innere Angelegenheiten".

Die einen morden in guter Ruh,
sind geheiligt, sind tabu –
Die andern flüstern und gucken zu.

MATILDA OLKINAITĖ

See the note for the poem 'During the Gnosiology Lesson', p. 29. The following poem is dated 26 November 1938.

MY PEOPLE

A pair of dark eyes ignited once again
With a pain that cannot be extinguished.
And they – they just keep walking past and away.
But for me, Lord, there are no words.

Do you hear? Do hear that awful laughter?
The hills, even the hills shake from it –
And the rivers will faint, and the seas will faint –
And the stone will cry, the stone will cry.

You are laughing? You walk past and keep on walking,
But for me, Lord, there are no words for my horror.
That laughter – that awful laughter… And dark eyes flash
With an undying, relentless pain.

Translated from the Lithuanian by Laima Vincė

MANO TAUTA

Dvi juodos akys vėl užsiliepsnojo
Negęstančiu, nemirštančiu skausmu
O jie – pro šalį eina ir praeina,
O man, o Viešpatie, taip neapsakoma.

Jūs girdit? Girdit klaikų juoką?
Kalnai, kalnai drebės nuo jo –
Ir upės alps, ir jūros alps –
Ir verks akmuo, ir verks akmuo.

Jūs juokiatės? Jūs einat ir praeinat
O man, o Viešpatie, taip neapsakomai baugu
Tas juokas – toks klaikus… Ir akys juodos dega
Negęstančiu, nemirštančiu skausmu.

ALFRED KERR

See the note preceding 'World in Turmoil ...', p. 33. Kerr had fled Germany with his wife and children in 1933 and they settled in England in 1935, where he wrote this poem in 1936. His daughter was the well-known children's author, Judith Kerr, who died in 2019.

THE MOST AFFLICTED

Of all who are hated and harried and hurt
The Jews get it worst, they are treated like dirt.
And not for hatching political plots –
But just for existing, more often than not.

Translated from the German by Jean Boase-Beier

DAS SCHLIMMSTE

Die Juden haben unbestritten
Von allen Verfolgten das Schlimmste gelitten:
Nicht weil sie politisch verschworen sind –
Nur weil sie halt geboren sind.

JAN CAMPERT

Campert, a Dutch writer and critic, published this poem in 1933 as a direct reaction to the Nazi book burnings. He was later interned in Neuengamme Concentration Camp for helping Jews escape to Belgium, and died there in 1943.

BALLAD OF THE BURNING BOOKS

They laid licentious hands on us,
their mindless bragging reached the skies,
they burned us on a blazing pyre,
with each book burned an artist died.
They threw us in their grimy wagons,
drove them past laughing hordes to a square
where our Comrade Hans Heinz Ewers
sat enthroned in his Hallowed Chair.

– Fallada, may the flames devour you! –
WHO WILL FORGET LÄMMCHEN EVER?

They stole us from the library shelves,
compiled with effort down the years;
a horde of know-nothings out for revenge
dared to lay their hands on us.
The common folk in streets and squares
blind and mad, with no holds barred,
a pack of foolish little people
greets this folly with shouts of *Heil*!

– Of Thomas Mann only ashes still remain! –
BUT THE BUDDENBROOKS SURVIVED THE FLAMES!

The dreams that once inspired the best,
The joy and sorrow we turned to words,
the work for which thousands paid respect,
the voices everyone had heard,
they tried to wipe them out for ever,
they created a monstrous *auto da fé*…
Listen, comrades, the fierce flames roar,
they carry off your disgrace!

– Fire, carry off the works of Wassermann! –
JUNKER ERNST HE STILL REMAINS!

And everywhere in the German lands,
in every village, each small town
there was a square where high command
decreed our pyres, our ashes trod down,
a Mouth was there which knew not what it said,
a Hand, which knew not what it did…
Forgive this people when in times to come
they see the evil they have done!

– Your *Reich*, Arnold Zweig, is gone within the hour –
GRISCHA WAS FACED WITH FIERCER FIRES!

The smoke contracts to a black cloud,
the wind disperses the poor remains;
the work is gone, and gone the names,
that once were the flower of this land.
The gentlemen who know things better,
noisily celebrate the symbolic Feast,
one thing to their shame is forgotten:
inviolable, the honest soul!

THOMAS MANN, FALLADA, WASSERMANN, ZWEIG
HAVE ALREADY ATTAINED THE ETERNAL *REICH*!

Translated from the Dutch by Donald Gardner

BALLADE DER VERBRANDE BOEKEN

Zij grepen naar ons met schennende handen,
de lucht was vervuld van hun brallend woord,
zij gingen ons allen tezamen verbranden,
met ieder boek werd een kunst'naar vermoord.
Op smerige karren heeft men ons gesmeten,
die reden door rijen van hoon en gejoel
naar een plein waar Genosse Hans Heinz Ewers
zat op zijn Heilige, Zuivere Stoel.

– Fallada, mogen de vlammen je vreten! –
WIE ZAL LÄMMCHEN VERGETEN?

Zij roofden ons weg uit bibliotheken,
zo moeizaam in lange jaren ontstaan;
een horde wraakzuchtige, dwaze leken
bestond het aan ons de handen te slaan.
Het volk in de straten en op de pleinen,
verblind en bezeten, tot alles bereid,
de bende der talloos Onnozele Kleinen
verheerlijkt met Heil's deze Stommiteit!

– Van Thomas Mann is slechts as gebleven! –
MAAR DE BUDDENBROOKS LEVEN!

De dromen, die de besten eens bezielden,
het Lief en Leed dat ons werd tot woord,
het werk, waardoor de duizenden eens knielden,
de stemmen naar wie elkeen heeft gehoord,
men trachtte hen voor altijd uit te roeien,
men richtte aan een groots auto da fé…
Genossen hört, de felle vlammen loeien,
zij nemen al uw schande met zich mee!

– Vuur, neem de werken van Wassermann aan! –
JUNKER ERNST BLIJFT TOCH BESTAAN!

En overal in de Germaanse landen,
in ieder dorp, in elke kleine stad
was er een plein, waar wij op hoog bevel verbrandden
en waar men onze as met voeten trad,
was er een Mond, die niet wist wat hij zeide,
was er een Hand, die niet wist wat zij deed…
Vergeef dit volk als het in andere tijden
zijn eigen blinde Euveldaden weet!

– Geen uur, Arnold Zweig, zal je rijk meer duren –
GRISCHA STOND VOOR HETER VUREN!

De rook trekt tot een donk're wolk te zamen,
de wind verwaait het povere restant;
vergaan het werk, vergaan de vele namen,
die waren eens de glorie van dit land.
De heren, die het alles beter weten,
vieren luidruchtig het symbolisch Feest,
maar één ding werd tot eigen schâ vergeten:
dat onaanrandbaar is: de goede geest!

THOMAS MANN, FALLADA, WASSERMANN, ZWEIG
WONNEN REEDS DAS EWIGE REICH!

MARGARETE SUSMAN

Susman, born in 1872 in Hamburg, was a critic, essayist, poet and dramatist. She went as a child to live in Switzerland with her family. After studying in Germany, she left in 1933, never to return, and died in Zurich in 1966. She wrote this poem in 1936.

WE WANDER

We wander, we wander
No end in sight, no goal
No pictures or parables call,
We of all people on earth
Forever the Other.

From humanity's darkest pain
We greet you as we wander,
In death we are the same
And only in life the Other.

Translated from the German by Jean Boase-Beier

WIR WANDERN

Wir wandern, wir wandern,
Nicht Ziel noch Ende gilt,
Wo Gleichnis nicht winkt noch Bild,
Wir, unter den Völkern der Welt
Die ewig Andern.

Aus des Menschseins dunkelster Not,
Wir grüßen euch nur im Wandern
Verbunden im gleichen Tod
Und nur im Leben die Andern.

II
LIFE IN GHETTOS, CAMPS, PRISONS AND
THE OUTSIDE WORLD

RAJZEL ZYCHLINSKI

Yiddish poet Zychlinski was born in 1910 in Gabin, Poland and died in 2001 in Concord, California. Though this poem was written in 1947 in the Polish city of Łódź, it takes the point of view of someone imprisoned, perhaps in the ghetto.

PRAYER

earth,
let me know once more
the scent of your grass
and the rushing of trees
in your forests, –
let me swim once more
to the light-filled banks.
let the still grey bark of your pines
be my friend again.
for now it all is drowning
in blood-filled fog.
the leaves scream,
and the sun pierces.

earth,
let me know once more
the scent of your grass.

Translated from the Yiddish by Jean Boase-Beier

TFILE

erd,
los mich nochamol derfiln
dem rejech fun dajne grosn,
mitn rojschn fun di bejmer
in dajne welder, –
los mich wider schwimen
tsu lojtere bregn.
sol wider sajn frajntlech tsu mir
di groje kore fun dajne sosnes.
wajl alts trinkt sich

in a blutikn nepl.
di bleter schrajen,
un di sun schtecht.

erd,
los mich nochamol derfiln
dem rejech fun deine grosn.

H. G. ADLER

Adler was born in Prague in 1910. In 1942 he was imprisoned in Terezín (or Theresienstadt), a former military base 30 km north of Prague, transformed by the Germans in 1941 into a ghetto.

AMONG MURDERED SOULS

Among murdered souls,
Can you hear?
The cheers of the Evil One.
How he twists
In the tangle of breathing corpses.
The night swallows cold.
Cobbled of screams and moans,
The terrible open hatred of brothers;
Oh, the night,
Without comfort,
Without the comforting scent
Of long-lived age.

Can you hear?
Harder and harder
The cursed torch of anger
Is swung with a roar;
Whoever is hit
Is wiped out
From all memory,
Swallowed by forgetting
Down! Down
Into slime and decay!

Speak! Speak! – No,
Spit out falling cries
So that up there – that one – the eternal… –
But no –
Keep quiet!
Not a move,
Just hide your most lonely light
In silent hope –

Among murdered souls,
Do you hear?
Welcome your fate!

Translated from the German by Jean Boase-Beier

UNTER GEMORDETEN SEELEN

Unter gemordeten Seelen,
Hörst du es?,
Das Jauchzen des Bösen?
Wie er sich windet
Im Gewinde der atmenden Leichen!
Kalt schluckt die Nacht.
Aus schreienden Seufzern gemischt,
Den furchtbar verwegenen Bruderhaß;
O – die Nacht –
Ohne Trost,
Ohne behaglichen Duft
Verweilender Reife.

Hörst du es?
Immer gewaltiger
Wird die Fluchfackel des Zornes
Dröhnend geschwungen;
Wen sie trifft,
Der ist gelöscht
Aus allem Gedächtnis,
Den schlürft das Vergessen
Hinab!, hinab
In Verwesung und Schlamm!

Sprich! sprich! – Nein,
Stürzende Schreie sprudle hinaus,
Daß oben – jener – der ewige… –

Doch, nein –
Verstumme!
Rühre dich nicht
Und verhülle dein einsamstes Licht
In stumme Erwartung –

Unter gemordeten Seelen,
Hörst du es?:
Liebe dein Schicksal!

JERZY OGÓREK Z BĘDZINA

Written in the Kraków ghetto in 1942, by an 11-year-old boy, this poem is a rewriting of the famous children's poem 'Lokomotywa' by the Polish author J. Tuwim, first published in 1936.

THE LOCOMOTIVE

I pay for my good heart with this simple verse on the day of my birthday

In the station stands an engine
Heavy and monstrous, sweat streaming down
Thick olive oil
It stands and gasps, breathes and blows
The glow from its warm body flows.
Oh, how hot,
Oh, how hot.
Now barely gasping,
Now barely puffing
And then the stoker pours the coal in.
Carriages attached behind it
Heavy monsters of wood and steel.
And every carriage full of *häftlings*
The Germans pile them in like horses.
Forty carriages perhaps in all,
Sixty *häftlings* in every one.
In every carriage children
Small and thin
It brings tears to your eyes.
They sit and keep quiet

As though nothing is wrong.
Then suddenly
A loud whistle sounds
Suddenly a hiss
Steam escapes
The wheels start up,
Slowly at first
Tortoise-heavy
The machine moves
Slowly on the rails
Pulling carriages
Dragging them slowly
Turning, turning
Wheel after wheel
The motion speeds up
Faster and faster
It taps
And knocks
And surges forward
But where to?
But where to?
Where is it going?
Through fields
Through forests

To Auschwitz

Translated from the Polish by Jean Boase-Beier with Dieter Beier

LOKOMOTYWA

Za dobre serce płacę nędznym wierszem w dniu urodzin

Stoi na stacji lokomotywa
Ciężka ogromna i pot z niej spływa
Tłusta oliwa
Stoi i sapie, dyszy i dmucha
Żar z rozgrzanego jej brzucha bucha.
Uf jak gorąco,
Uf jak gorąco.
Już ledwo sapie,

Już ledwo zipie
A jeszcze palacz w nią węgiel sypie.
Wagony do niej podoczepiali
Ciężkie, ogromne z drzewa i stali.
A pełno Häftlingów w każdym wagonie
Niemcy ładują ich przecież jak konie.
A tych wagonów może czterdzieści
W każdym sześćdziesiąt Häftlingów się mieści.
W każdym wagonie jest kilka dzieci,
Małe wychudłe
Aż łza do oka leci.
Siedzą spokojnie
Jak nigdy nic
A nagle
Słychać wielki gwizd
Nagle świst,
Para bucha,
Koła w ruch,
Najpierw powoli
Jak żółw ociężale
Ruszyła maszyna
Po szynach ospale
Szarpnęła wagony
Ciągnie z mozołem
Kręci się kręci
Koło za kołem
Biegu przyspiesza
I coraz prędzej
Stuka
Puka
Mocno i pędzi
A dokąd?
A dokąd?
A dokąd tak gna?
Przez pola
Przez lasy

Do Oświęcimia

H. G. ADLER

See the note on Adler before 'Among Murdered Souls', p. 44. Like that poem, this, too, was written in the ghetto at Terezín. Adler was subsequently sent to Auschwitz. He survived, and settled in England, where he died in 1988.

ARRIVAL OF THE OLD PEOPLE

Crowding round they stamp and swamp the yard,
And through them wheezes the rattling cart,
Swaying beneath its load of bones,
In the pressing throng so oddly alone.

The rickety ladder is brought up near,
Calls ring out, they can sense the fear,
The crooked gaze of wrinkled heads,
The trembling bundles timidly held.

Fingers fumble, a helper's arms reach out
Towards them then, to grab the meagre load.
In deathlike slumber heads loll back,
The bier creaks, dishevelled blankets slide.

Two bearers drag the load aslant the mud
Almost drowning there amongst the crowd.
The lackey passes, threatening with his gun,
Caps come raggedly off and eyes look down.

Translated from the German by Jean Boase-Beier

ANKUNFT DER GREISE

Der Hof schwirrt grell voll stampfendem Gedränge,
Schon keucht das rasselnde Gefährt
Und schwankt, von Knochenfracht beschwert,
Unfaßbar einsam in beklemmter Enge.

Die Rumpelstiege wird herangeschoben,
Zurufe klirren, Angst wird laut,
Das Runzelhaupt verbogen schaut,
Und zitternd wird das Bündel zag gehoben.

Die Hände nesteln, Helferarme strecken
Sich lang und fangen magre Last,
Der Kopf sackt ab zu toter Rast,
Es ächzt die Bahre, schütter fallen Decken.

Zwei Träger schleppen schief und sie ertrinken
In Gafferzeilen fast im Kot.
Der Scherge geht, die Waffe droht,
Die Kappen fallen schlaff, und Blicke sinken.

DAGMAR HILAROVÁ

*Hilarová wrote this poem as a teenager in the Terezín ghetto. The original
Czech text was never published. Lack of interest from her native country
after the war meant that Hilarová's ghetto poems were first published in
German, translated from Czech by Rudolf Iltis and Günther Deicke.*

WINDY NIGHT

Windy night.
Under window-eyes the alley flows,
Furrowed by the hot tracks
Of the human herd.

Landscape, forgive.
On our shoulders we bear your sorrow, too.
We go,
Our eyes gouged out
By submission to Fate,
Each burdened with their own.

Windy night.
Even the moon does not make a dog whimper.
No star fulfils
Our wish by its fall:
Like a bird with wounded wings
To lie down,
And not to wait for morning.

Translated from the German by Philip Wilson

WINDIGE NACHT

Windige Nacht.
Unter Fensteraugen rinnt die Gasse
Zerfurcht von den heißen Spuren
Der Menschenherde.
Landschaft, verzeih.
Auf den Schultern tragen wir auch dein Leid.
Wir gehen,
Die Augen ausgestochen
Von Schicksalsergebenheit,
Jeder beschwert mit dem Seinen.

Windige Nacht.
Selbst einen Hund bringt der Mond nicht zum Winseln.
Kein Stern erfüllt
Durch seinen Fall unsren Wunsch:
Wie ein Vogel mit wunden Schwingen
Sich hinzulegen
Und den Morgen nicht abzuwarten.

ABRAHAM SUTZKEVER

Jewish women were not allowed to give birth in the Vilnius ghetto. Abraham and Frejdke Sutzkever hid their newborn son, but the baby was found and murdered by the Nazis. Sutzkever wrote 'Vilnius Ghetto, 18 January 1943' beneath this poem. The Sutzkevers survived, and Abraham died in Tel Aviv in 2010.

TO THE CHILD

Whether out of hunger
Or just out of love
– the only witness was your mother –
I wanted to engulf you, my child,
to feel how your tiny body grew cold
in my fingers,
as though I held fast in them
a warm glass of tea
and felt its transition to cold.

For you are not just a stranger, not just a guest,
in our world we cannot give birth to another –,
we give ourselves birth, like a ring,
and these rings all join into chains.

Child of mine,
you whose spoken name means love,
and without words are that yourself,
you – the centre of all my dreams,
the hidden third one,
who from the ends of the earth
in the miracle of an invisible storm
brought and melded two together,
so they could give you life and joy:

why have you made this life go dark,
with the closing of your eyes
and left me here, poor as a beggar, out in the cold,
with a world, a snowbound world,
you have cast off, thrown me back?

Never did a cradle give you joy,
that in every movement
carries within it the rhythm of the stars.
The sun might as well shatter into pieces like glass,
for never have you seen its shining glow.
A drop of poison burnt the belief out of you
for you believed:
it was only sweet-warm milk.

*

I wanted to engulf you, my child.
So might I have felt the taste
of my hope's future.
Perhaps one day you will blossom
in my blood.

But no, I am not worthy to be your grave.
And so I will give you
to the snow that is calling,
to the snow, that marked for me the first holy day,
and you will sink
like a splinter of sunset
into its silent depths
and will carry a greeting from me
to the frozen grasses –

Translated from the Yiddish by Jean Boase-Beier

TSUM KINT

Tsi fun hunger,
tsi fun groyser libshaft,
nor an eydes iz derbay dayn mame:
ikh hob gevolt dikh aynshlingen, mayn kint,
baym filn vi dayn gufl kilt zikh op
in mayne finger,
glaykh ikh volt in zey gedrikt
a vareme gloz tey,
filndik dem ibergang tsu kaltkeyt.

Vayl du bist nit keyn fremder, nit keyn gast,
oyf unzer erd geboyrt men nit keyn tsveytn,
zikh aleyn geboyrt men vi a ring,
un di ringn shlisn zikh in keytn.

Kint mayns,
vos in verter heystu: libshaft,
un nit in verter bistu es aleyn,
du der kern fun mayn yede kholem,
farhoylener driter,
vos fun di veltishe vinklen
hostu mitn vunder fun an umgezeyenem shturem
tsunoyfgebrakht, tsunoyfgegosn tsveyen
tsu bashafn dikh un tsu derfreyen:

Far vos hostu fartunklt dem bashaf,
mit dem vos du host tsugemakht di oygn
un gelost mikh betlerdik in droysn
tsuzamen mit a velt an oysgeshneyter,
vos du host opgevorfn oyf tsurik?

Dikh hot nit derfreyt keyn vig,
vos yeder ir bavegung
bahalt in zikh dem ritem fun di shtern.
Es meg di zun tsebreklen zikh vi a gloz
vayl keyn mol hostu nit gezen ir shayn.
A tropn sam hot oysgebrent dayn gloybn.
Du host gemeynt:
s'iz varm-zise milkh.

*

Ikh hob gevolt dikh aynshlingen, mayn kint,
kedey tsu filn dem geshmak
fun mayn gehofter tsukunft.
Efsher vestu bliyen vi a mol
in mayn gebliyt.

Nor ikh bin nit vert tsu dayn keyver.
Vel ikh dikh avekshenken
dem rufindik shney,
dem shney mayn ershte yontev,
un vestu zinken
vi a shpliter zunfargang
in zayne shtile tifn
un opgebn a grus fun mir
di ayngefrirte grezelekh –

MELANIA FOGELBAUM

Fogelbaum, born in 1911, was a poet and painter, who was forced into the Łódź ghetto in 1940, along with her mother. After her deportation to Auschwitz, where she was sent to the gas chamber in August 1944, Nachman Zonabend found the notebooks containing her poems in the ghetto.

SPRING EVENING

The glassy sky-blue wind
Still turning its eyes back to winter
They are young, and thickly breathing stars
in the black room
the moon

a cold empty tear behind which is no pain
does not want to have flowed
into the congealed grey flower of the heart

Translated from the Polish by Jean Boase-Beier with Dieter Beier

WIECZÓR WIOSENNY

Szklany błękitny wiatr
Zwracając jeszcze oczy w zimę
Już młode, rzęsiście oddycha gwiazdami
w czarnym pokoju
księżyc
zimną pustą łzą za którą nie ma bólu
nie chce spłynąć
w szary, stężały kwiat serca

IN THE FRAGMENTS OF THE RUINS...

In the fragments of the ruins wrapped in wire
life hiccups, the stink of mouldy soup
in lice-filled straw of hair do not forget
children's eyes
that play with darkness
dull hunger sticks fast
scabs of dreams up to the swamp of floors
(behind the windows once, ten times, a hundred times a day
the corpses crept out to live)

Translated from the Polish by Jean Boase-Beier with Dieter Beier

W SKORUPACH RUDER...

W skorupach ruder owiniętych drutem
życie czka smród spleśniałej zupy
w zawszonym sitowiu włosów nie zapomnij
dziecięcych oczu
bawią się mrokiem
kołowaty głód przylepia
strupy snów do bagniska podłóg
(za oknami raz, dziesięć, sto na dzień
wypełzły po życie trupy)

ANONYMOUS

This poem was written in the Auschwitz-Birkenau 'Zigeunerlager' (Gypsy Camp).

SONG OF THE ROMA

Do not wake me from my dream,
so the world need never know
how they treat a Roma.

My dearest girl, do not look,
so you need not see
how they treat a Roma.
God lets no joy come into our homes.

My girl, think of the honour
that once was ours.
But no more fire,
no joy, no laughter.

Soon nothing but night,
and no day, only in dreams.

Translated from the German by Jean Boase-Beier

LIED DER ROMA

Weckt mich nicht aus meinem Traum,
damit diese Welt nicht verstehen muß
wie ein Rom behandelt wird.

Liebes Mädchen, schau nicht hin,
damit Du nicht sehen mußt
wie ein Rom behandelt wird.
Gott gibt nicht, daß Freude bei uns einkehrt.

Mädchen, sieh' die Würde,
Die wir einst hatten.
Es gibt kein Feuer mehr,
Freude und Lachen.

Bald wird nur noch Nacht sein,
Tag nur noch Traum.

JAN CAMPERT

This poem was written in 1941, before Campert's arrest and internment in 1942. See the note above 'Ballad of the Burning Books', p. 36.

THE THREE REFUGEES

It was the woman I saw first;
I'm just that sort of man.
Her face was wrinkled like a map
of mountainous terrain.
What verdict human or from hell
had damned her beyond return?

Under her headscarf her grey locks
hung limply round her brow;
she stood there deadly weary, like
someone loitering, lost
on the corner of a suburban street
in snow and wintry frost.

She didn't turn and look at the man
with a parcel in his hand.
He has to be her son, I guessed,
they're at their journey's end
and don't know what's in store for them
in this my native land.

In his left hand he held the parcel
in faded paper tied;
on his right there stood a thin young girl,
wearing a red beret, while fear
gleamed in her anxious eyes that asked,
what am I doing here?

He seemed to be speaking to the woman,
but she just strode ahead.
Words like 'we've still some way to go...',
but, lost in her dreams, she paid no heed
to his timorous warning but walked on
further as if asleep.

They crossed the platform as I watched –
man, woman, child – to where
Amsterdam the city begins,
out of the station, down the stairs…
The sun was shining on the water
and spring was in the air.

He laid his parcel on the ground
and blinked in the morning light;
the woman pulled herself together,
and buttoned her child's coat tight;
and I who had stood just next to them
left with a poem to write.

Translated from the Dutch by Donald Gardner

DE DRIE VLUCHTELINGEN

Het eerst zag ik de vrouw, dat ligt
nu eenmaal in mijn aard.
Hoe gerimpeld was haar gezicht
(een berglandschap in kaart).
Door welk hels en aards gericht
werd haar geen leed bespaard?

Onder de doek rond het gelaat
sliertten wat haren grauw;
zij stond daar als ene die staat
– een doodvermoeide vrouw –
op de hoek van een voorstadsstraat
in sneeuw en winterkou.

Zij keek niet om naar de man,
een pak in de ene hand.
Ik dacht: dit is haar zoon. En dàn:
zij zijn zeker hier gestrand
en zij weten niet wat er van
hen worden moet in mijn land.

In de ene hand het pakket
gewikkeld in vaal papier;
ter rechter met rode baret
een mager meisje, wier
verwilderde ogen ontzet
vroegen: wat doe ik hier?

Het leek of de man wat zei aan
de vrouw, die voor hen liep.
Misschien: wij moeten verder gaan…
En zij, in dromen diep,
hoorde nauw zijn schuchter vermaan
en ging alsof zij sliep.

Ik volgde hen over 't perron
– de vrouw, de man, het kind –
de trap af en uit het station…
Waar Amsterdam begint
scheen over het water de zon
en woei een voorjaarswind.

De man lei het pak op de grond
en knipperde in het licht;
de vrouw, die zichzelve hervond,
knoopte het jasje dicht
van het kind; ik die bij hen stond
liep door met dit gedicht.

MIRCEA LACATUS

Lacatus is a Roma sculptor and poet from Transylvania, in Romania. He was given asylum in Austria in 1990, after his participation in the student protests for democracy in Bucharest. He also lives part of the time in the United States.

MY LOVE

don't worry
i'm alright here we have everything
there isn't much food but it tastes good
the officers care about us
they don't beat us don't swear at us
sometimes we trip when we are working
and fall down and no one kicks us with their boots
in our back in our ribs in our mouth it's good over here
if only you weren't so far away and i knew that you are well
i keep thinking about when we meet again
your reaction when you see i am almost a skeleton

i am hollowed out from missing you
but soon i will be back on my feet
when your warm body is hugging me each night
and your quiet voice is reading gently to my ear
poems by rilke

Translated from the Romanian by Roman-Gabriel Olar & Marian de Vooght

IUBITA MEA

să nu fii îngrijorată
mi-e bine aici e cald avem de toate
mâncarea nu multă dar e gustoasă
ofițerii sunt atenți cu noi
nu ne bat nu ne înjură
uneori la muncă ne mai împiedicăm
si cădem și nimeni nu ne lovește cu bocancii
în spate în coaste în gură e bine aici
numai de nu ai fi atât e departe și de aș știi că ești bine
mă tot gândesc la întalnirea noastră
ce o să zici când vei vedea că am ajuns aproape un schelet
numai dorul de tine m-a pustiit
dan repede am să mă pun pe picioare
când voi simti trupul tău cald îmbrățișându-mă în fiecare seară
și vocea ta moale citindu-mi încet la ureche
poeme din rilke

MAURICE HONEL

*Honel, born in Paris in 1903, was a Communist politician, involved
in resistance to the Nazis. This poem was written in 1948, and recalls
Honel's forced labour in Auschwitz. He survived Auschwitz, and died in
Paris in 1977.*

DANCE AT COMMAND GROUP HOLTZMANN

In the September fog
There was evening mist
In the cement dust
There was the haggard gaze of useless-faced men
In the fixed eye of the projectors
There were fifty compulsory kilos to carry
There was the teeth-chattering dry cold

The stomach-yawning hunger
The memories of those still walking with a nanny
The certainty given by the good faith of vertigo
The shovel of bottomless holes
The sucking crane
The trucks in perpetual motion
The Kapo smoking our bread for four
The coal – abstracted – from the mine
Our – clinging – to the camp's electrified recesses
In the world of so much per cent
We were twenty out of a thousand
Still alive
Feeble minus-values.
To dance in the September fog
In perpetual coal
In the circus of crematoria.

Translated from the French by Timothy Adès

DANSE AU KOMMANDO HOLTZMANN

Dans le brouillard de septembre
Il y avait la brume du soir
Dans la poussière du ciment
Il y avait l'œil hagard des hommes aux faces inutiles.
Dans l'œil fixe des projecteurs
Il y avait cinquante kilos sur le dos indispensables.
Il y avait le froid sec qui claque des dents
La faim qui fait bâiller le ventre
Les souvenirs de ceux qui marchaient encore avec une nourrice
La certitude que donne la bonne foi du vertige
Il y avait la pelle des trous sans fond
La grue suceuse
Les wagonnets du mouvement perpétuel
Le Kapo qui fumait notre pain pour quatre
Le charbon – détaché – de la mine
Notre – adhésion – aux profondeurs électrifiées du camp
Dans le monde du tant pour cent
Nous étions vingt pour mille
Restés vivants
Moins-values débiles.
À danser dans le brouillard de septembre
Dans le charbon perpétuel
Au cirque des crématoires.

CHARLOTTE SERRE

This poem was written in Ravensbrück, where Serre was imprisoned from January 1944 until April 1945. Together with her husband Charles she had led the Resistance in North Dordogne. Serre died in 2000.

CREMATORIUM

Avid flame-tongues lick black sky
Red fires hypnotise the eye
Burnt flesh smell invades you there
Acrid smoke plays out despair.

Translated from the French by Timothy Adès

CRÉMATOIRE

Langues de feu léchant avides le ciel noir
L'œil est hypnotisé par cette rouge flamme
L'odeur de chair roussie en vous creuse le drame
Se joue en la fumée âcre du désespoir.

IBOJA WANDALL-HOLM

Wandall-Holm was born in Czechoslovakia in 1923. She is a survivor of Auschwitz, Birkenau and Rajsko concentration camps and of a death march in 1945. She settled in Denmark with her second husband and began her writing career there in 1965.

FIELD WORK IN AUSCHWITZ

Breadovens
bird droppings
rattling roads
dust specks
seed burst
towers among sunflowers
guard
day after day
our
mute petrifaction

Translated from the Danish by Marian de Vooght

PÅ MARKARBEJDE I AUSCHWITZ

Brødovne
spurvedrys
klapreveje
støvfregner
frøblæst
tårne i solsikker
vogter
dagenes
vor
stumme forstening

FOSTY

The painter José Fosty, usually known only by his surname, was born in 1919 in Dalhem in Belgium. He wrote this poem in Buchenwald, where he was interned because of his involvement in the Belgian Resistance. Fosty donated the drawings he and his friend Paul Goyard made in the concentration camp to the Buchenwald Memorial Site. He died in 2015.

THE FOREST IN CHAINS

The fairies run away. Axemen, accursed, invade
    the clearing where their dancing circles played:

Blows ring throughout the forest, echoing again
    like dark forebodings in a prisoner's brain.

And what was just now green and fey and mischievous
    is slowly stripped, a kind of charnel-house.

The clearing grows and grows, a hollow in the verdure,
    showing the sky a scar that still gapes wider.

The camp is built as the lash falls on bleeding backs,
    as fir-trees writhe and bleed beneath the axe.

Over the sufferers, relentless terror reigns:
    winter and fear and hunger are their chains.

God's holy fools in old times recognised their doom:
  this age has holy fools for martyrdom.

They learn, with banners like a living lantern-light,
  to live and die for revellers' delight.

Translated from the French by Timothy Adès

LA FORÊT ENCHAÎNÉE

Lorsque les fées s'enfuient les damnés bûcherons
Envahissent la clairière où elles dansaient en rond.

Au sein de la forêt la hache a résonné
Comme un mauvais présage au cœur de l'interné.

Et celle qui fut jadis riante de verdure
S'est pelée peu à peu comme une sépulture.

La clairière s'élargit, clairière toujours si verte
Ne montrant plus au ciel qu'une plaie plus ouverte.

Et le camp se bâtit sous les coups de cravaches,
Tandis que les sapins se tordaient sous la hache.

La terreur sans cesse régnait sur les damnés
Le froid, la faim, la peur les tenant enchaînés.

Comme les fous de Dieu jadis savaient mourir,
D'autres fous de ce siècle devenaient des martyrs.

Élevant leurs drapeaux comme un vivant fanal
Ils sauront vivre et mourir pour que plus beau soit le bal.

CHARLOTTE SERRE

This poem was written in Ravensbrück. See the note on Serre's poem 'Crematorium', p. 62.

THE CAMP

Horror, terror, hunger, blows,
Flames, the walls, the whip, the cold,
Lice and roll-call, dogs and snow...

The watch-tower...

Turn... turn... carousel...

Translated from the French by Timothy Adès

LE CAMP

L'horreur, l'effroi, les coups, la faim,
Le feu, les murs, le fouet, les chiens,
Les poux, le froid, l'appel, la neige,

Le mirador...

Que tourne... tourne... le manège...

RENÉ BLIECK

Blieck was born in Brussels in 1910, and imprisoned in Neuengamme concentration camp as a Communist, active in the Belgian Resistance. He wrote this poem for the wife of Pierre de Tollenaere, who was hanged on 6 December 1944. Blieck was killed on the Nazi prison ship Cap Ancona, sunk by the British Air Force in May 1945.

IF SLOWLY YOU GO TO A LONELY PLACE...

If slowly you go to a lonely place,
kneel without noise, and pray for a moment...
then please add my name to the flight of your prayer.

And grave, recollected, invoking the past,
forgetting yourself, your eyes raised to heaven,
you'll see my frozen heart drift.

Come at the hour when day falls.
My heart will still tremble if it hears you
murmur: I love you, friend.

And if joyful spring breaks out one morning
with rosy buds on a desolate mound,
raise them to your lips – friend.

Beyond the grave, kisses can still
be exchanged …

Translated from the French by Philip Wilson

IRAS-TU, LENTEMENT DANS UN LIEU SOLITAIRE...

Iras-tu, lentement dans un lieu solitaire
t'agenouiller sans bruit et prier un instant?
Mêleras-tu mon nom au vol de ta prière?

Et grave et recueillie invoquant le passé,
t'oublieras-tu, les yeux attachés sur le ciel
où flottera mon cœur glacé?

Viens à l'heure où le jour tombe.
Mon cœur tressaillira encore s'il t'entend
murmurer: je t'aime encore amie.

Et si le gai printemps un matin fait éclore
sur un tertre désert quelques boutons rosés,
porte-les à ta lèvre – amie.

On peut encore au-delà de la tombe
échanger des baisers...

CATHERINE ROUX

Roux was born in Lyon in 1918. This poem was written in Ravensbrück, where Roux was imprisoned from 1944-1945 as a member of the French Resistance.

MY GOD

(After the search on arrival at Ravensbrück, 22 April 1944)

My God,
I've no clothes on me now
I've no shoes
I've no bag, no notecase, no pen,
I've no name. I've been labelled 35282.
I've no hair, I've no hanky,
I've no photos of mother and my nephews now.
I've not got the anthology from which every day in my cell in
    Fresnes I learnt a poem.
I've got nothing now. My skull, my body, my hands are naked.
    Boche! Search, Strip, Rob, Shave, Degrade my person.
Arm my hands with shovels and pickaxes.
Make me into a woodcutter, a ditch-digger, a tipper of excrement, a
    snow-sweeper, a convict labouring in the bog.
Sculpt my face, my wrinkles, my body so I look like thousands on
    thousands of woman prisoners.
Give my eyes that frightening fixed glare that I often see, with
    horror, in the eyes of my companions.
Deafen my ears with your shouting.
Wield your bludgeon.
Kick with your booted feet.
Murderess, pile our starved bodies by day and night into your
    crematoria.
Show our eyes the inhuman spectacle of women dying like
    animals, there in a corner!
Without ever stopping: beat, wound, hang, shoot.
Boche, since childhood, my Country, which is France, has clothed
    me with wool of its sheep, flax of its fields, silk of its insects.

To my ear, it has granted the sea's music and the wind's breath, soft
   or stormy. It has brought me to its mountain peaks, to the purity
   of eternal snows.
I've seemed to rediscover the faraway soul that I had when the
   world began.
It has made me into a girl walking in the wind, my hair and spirit
   free; it has etched my brain, raised it up to the great voice of the
   masters.
It has civilized my heart, rid me of brute violence, educated my
   instincts, tuned my sensibility, moulded my courage, peopled
   my head with music, with poems, with words from books I love.
It has given me a mother and ringed me with sweet smiles of
   children.
My Country, which is France, has spread above me the gentleness,
   the tenderness, the calm of its sky.
In my heart, hated criminal Boche, wild beast still slobbering our
   blood, it has put a love so deep that in this place,
Imprisoned,
Unarmed,
Mother-naked,
I feel rich as a queen and I hold up my head with pride.

   Translated from the French by Timothy Adès

MON DIEU

   (Après la fouille d'entrée, Ravensbrück, 22 avril 1944)

   Mon Dieu,
   Je n'ai plus de vêtements sur moi,
   Je n'ai plus de chaussures,
   Je n'ai plus de sac, de portefeuille, de stylo,
   Je n'ai plus de nom. On m'a étiquetée 35202.
   Je n'ai plus de cheveux,
   Je n'ai plus de mouchoir,
   Je n'ai plus de photos de maman et de mes neveux,
   Je n'ai plus l'anthologie où, chaque jour, dans ma cellule de
      Fresnes, j'apprenais ma poésie,
   Je n'ai plus rien. Mon crâne, mon corps, mes mains sont
      nues. Boche! Dénude, Fouille, Pille, Rase, Animalise ma
      silhouette,
   Arme mes mains de pelles et de pioches ;
   Fais de moi une bûcheronne, une terrassière, une videuse

d'excréments, une déblayeuse de neige, une forçate des marais.

Sculpte mon visage, mes rides, mon corps pour que je ressemble à des milliers et des milliers de prisonnières.

Donne à mes yeux cette fixité effrayante que je retrouve, horrifiée, dans les yeux de mes compagnes.

Assourdis mes oreilles par tes hurlements.

Manie le gourdin

Donne des coups de bottes.

Assassine, emplis jour et nuit avec nos pauvres corps d'affamées tes krématoriums

Mets devant nos yeux le spectacle inhumain de celles qui meurent comme des bêtes, là dans un coin !

Sans t'arrêter jamais, matraque, blesse, pend, fusille !

Boche, depuis l'enfance, mon Pays, qui est la France, m'a vêtu de la laine de ses moutons, du lin de ses champs, de la soie de ses insectes.

A mon oreille, il a accordé la musique des mers et le souffle du vent, douce ou tumultueuse. Il m'a conduite à la cime de ses montagnes et dans la pureté des neiges éternelles.

J'ai cru retrouver l'âme lointaine que j'eus au commencement de la terre.

Il a fait de moi une fille marchant dans le vent, les cheveux et l'esprit libres ; il a buriné mon cerveau, il l'a élevé jusqu'à la grande voix des maîtres.

Il a civilisé mon cœur, éloigné de moi la violence de la brute, éduqué mes instincts, harmonisé ma sensibilité, malaxé mon courage,

peuplé ma tête de musiques, de poèmes, de fragments de livres aimés.

Il m'a donné une mère et m'a entouré de doux sourires d'enfants.

Mon Pays, qui est la France, a tendu sur moi la douceur, la tendresse, la sérénité de son ciel.

Il a mis dans mon cœur, ô Boche haï, criminel, ô bête sauvage, encore toute bavante de notre sang, un amour si profond, que là,

Prisonnière,

Désarmée,

Toute nue,

Je me sens riche comme une reine, et que je relève hautement le front.

EDITH BRUCK

*Bruck was born in 1932, and is a survivor of Auschwitz, Dachau,
Christianstadt and Bergen-Belsen. Her parents and one brother died
in the camps. Originally from Hungary, she settled with her husband,
the poet Nelo Risi, in Rome in the 1950s.*

ARRIVAL

The system's womb has suddenly given birth
to twins by the million.
Its wheels filled with hate and authority
scream orders.
They appear out of the fog in their grey greatcoats
they thrash around wildly
they strike us blindly breaking up the line that has formed
with fists and kicks and rifle blows.
Our ears are deaf, the words
are swallowed by the wind
that carries from the death factories
the stench of charred flesh and ashes
on our heads, shaved for sins we have not committed.

Translated from the Italian by Peter Ualrig Kennedy

ARRIVO

Il grembo del sistema di colpo ha partorito
gemelli a milioni.
Le sue ruote gonfie di odio e di obbedienza
urlano ordini.
Sbucano dalle nebbie e le palandrane grigie
come impazzite si spostano in continuazione
ci colpiscono alla cieca rompendo la fila
guadagnata con pugni e calci e colpi di fucile.
Le orecchie sono sorde, le parole
le inghiotte il vento
che dalle fabbriche di morte
porta odore di carne bruciacchiata e cenere
sulle nostre teste calve di colpe non commesse.

ROBERT DESNOS

Desnos, born in Paris in 1900, worked for the Resistance until he was sent to Auschwitz, from where he was moved to Buchenwald, Flossenbürg and finally to Terezín, where he died in June, 1945, one month after liberation.

CHANT OF THE CURSE

– The curse is on you, the curse is on us! So they chant, the heroes that follow you.

– The curse is on you and none will dare touch you. Your life is damned and your person strikes murderers with dread.

– The curse is on you, the curse is on us, for we have revived ancient practices and prehistoric methods.

– The curse is on you and we wish only to be your barbarous tribe, obedient to your orders and dying without a word.

– The curse is on you, the curse is on us, therefore we have widened our circle on the earth around you.

– The curse is on you! Our conquests, bloody sacrifices, are the measure of our common madness, ours and yours.

– The curse is on you, the curse is on us! Wherever we can, we neglect architecture and deepen our cemeteries.

– The curse is on you and nothing can avail against you, our master! untouchable! the equal of lunatics, lepers and the plague-stricken.

– The curse is on you, the curse is on us! A monstrous death and nothing else detains us in its stalls and its abattoirs.

– The curse is on you, our master! gravedigger! and your people march to your call, towards the inexorable sacrifice.

– The curse is on you, the curse is on us. That food which you withhold from us, we cannot give you.

– The curse is on you and you will die of hunger, as we will, duly following the rite, and the peoples of the world will rejoice.

– The curse is on you, the curse is on us, ferocious beasts, executioners, idiots.

– The curse is on you! Adolf Hitler! Führer! Master! Very destiny of a people that has chosen to be criminal and hated.

– The curse is on you, the curse is on us! So they chant, the soldiers of death-racked Germany, the beast-faced, monkey-brained, swine-hearted soldiers of death-racked Germany.

– The curse is on you, the curse is on us! Nothing can free us from the tragic destiny we have chosen in you, we the German mob of lunatics who don't know we are already dead, starving vampires in search of putrescence and nothingness.

– The curse, the curse is on you, the curse is on us, and ruin and death, defeat and famine, and not so much as a legend of gold and of blood to ease our ghosts from their torment. The curse is on you, the curse is on us.

Translated from the French by Timothy Adès

CHANT DU TABOU

– Le tabou est sur toi, le tabou est sur nous ! Ainsi chantent les héros qui te suivent.

– Le tabou est sur toi et nul n'osera te toucher. Ta vie est sacrée et ta personne frappe d'épouvante les meurtriers.

– Le tabou est sur toi, le tabou est sur nous, car nous avons ravivé les anciennes coutumes et les usages préhistoriques.

– Le tabou est sur toi et nous ne voulons être que ta peuplade barbare, obéissant à tes ordres et mourant sans mot dire.

– Le tabou est sur toi, le tabou est sur nous, c'est pourquoi nous avons élargi, autour de toi, notre cercle sur la terre.

– Le tabou est sur toi ! Nos conquêtes, sanglants sacrifices, sont la mesure de notre commune folie, la tienne et la nôtre.

– Le tabou est sur toi, le tabou est sur nous ! Partout où nous passons nous creusons nos cimetières à la place des architectures.

– Le tabou est sur toi et nul ne peut rien contre toi, ô chef ! ô intouchable ! pareil aux déments, aux lépreux et aux pestiférés.

– Le tabou est sur toi, le tabou est sur nous ! Une mort magique nous garde, seule, dans ses étables et ses abattoirs.

– Le tabou est sur toi, ô chef ! ô fossoyeur ! et ton peuple marche à tes cris ver l'inexorable sacrifice.

– Le tabou est sur toi, le tabou est sur nous. La nourriture que tu nous refuses, nous ne pouvons te la donner.

– Le tabou est sur toi et tu mourras de faim, comme nous-mêmes, suivant le rite, et les peuples de la terre se réjouiront.

 – Le tabou est sur toi, le tabou est sur nous, bêtes cruelles, bourreaux, imbéciles.

– Le tabou est sur toi ! Adolphe Hitler ! Führer ! Chef ! Destin même d'un peuple qui a choisi d'être criminel et haï.

– Le tabou est sur toi, le tabou est sur nous ! Ainsi chantent les soldats de l'agonisante Allemagne, gueules de brutes, cervelles de singes, cœurs de porcs de l'agonisante Allemagne.

– Le tabou est sur toi, le tabou est sur nous ! Rien ne peut nous libérer du tragique destin que nous avons choisi en toi, nous, la foule allemande des déments et qui doutons de n'être pas morts déjà et vampires affamés en quête de pourriture et de néant.

– Le tabou, le tabou est sur toi, le tabou est sur nous et la
ruine et la mort, la défaite et la famine, et pas même une
légende d'or et de sang pour tirer nos ombres de leur
tourment. Le tabou est sur toi, le tabou est sur nous.

MÓNICA SIFRIM

*Born in Buenos Aires in 1958, Sifrim is a writer, translator and teacher of
creative writing. Oded Peled is one of Israel's 'second-generation' poets, a
child of Holocaust survivors.*

LETTERS FROM BERGEN-BELSEN

To Oded Peled

The post carried to Buenos Aires
letters from Bergen-Belsen
and postcards
of Bavarian meadows in bloom.

"We're fine" read the relatives'
shaky handwriting
sketchy as a dead man's.

And my mother, a little girl, smiled

imagining warm cake shops
that glazed the snow
smelling of chocolate.

"Due to limited space we have moved
to this place
where we find ourselves
in good health"

said the relatives
on the threshold of the crematorium.

And my mother gasped
imagining rivers of beer,
blond aunties draped in ermine,
skating cousins
perfuming the snow
with their songs, sledges and Tyrolean dresses.

"We look forward to hearing from you soon"

gasped the postcards
delivered to the tenement by a postman
as he struck up
a little waltz.

Translated from the Spanish by Cecilia Rossi

CARTAS DE BERGEN-BELSEN

A Oded Peled

El correo traía a Buenos Aires
cartas de Bergen-Belsen
y tarjetas postales
con las praderas bávaras en flor.

"Estamos bien" trazaban los parientes
con letra temblorosa
de difunto.

Y mi madre, pequeña, reía imaginando

tibias pastelerías
que flambeaban la nieve
de olor a chocolate.

"Nos hemos trasladado por razones
de espacio
a este lugar
donde nos encontramos
con salud"

decían los parientes
en el umbral del horno crematorio.

Y mi madre jadeaba
imaginando ríos de cerveza,
tías rubias forradas en armiño,
primas patinadoras
perfumando la nieve
con sus trinos, trineos y trajes del Tirol.

"Esperamos saber de ustedes pronto"

jadeaban las postales
que un cartero traía al conventillo
con pasitos
de vals.

ARNULF ØVERLAND

Øverland, an artist and poet born in Kristiansund in 1889, was imprisoned for his work in the Norwegian Resistance. He wrote this poem in the Sachsenhausen concentration camp. He died in Oslo in 1968.

THE DYSENTERY BARRACKS

He walks in with knees shaking,
he waits, just stands by the stove.
The smell is thick, his body and clothes
are wet with excrement.
They get a bucket, a dirty brown sponge,
and wash the man.
That's how he enters the final battle
and the bitter peace.

Three-tier bunk beds fill the ward,
fill it up to the ceiling.
A woollen blanket and a bag of straw
are all you need here.
You wanted more, my friend,
so here's your bowl for soup.
And the days, the ones that remain,
you just will have to bear.

He lies there looking pale as death,
his bony fists all covered in a rash.
He gets up and wants to walk,
you can see that he's alive.
That's surely what he'd meant to do;
but he drifts off and cannot talk.
In the sheet they lift him, carry him away,
now there's space for someone new.

Life comes to an end in ways
you had never expected.
To the last minute it entices
with rewards you didn't get.
A garden opens like a miracle,
it's playing in the gilded linden;
and the apples are that golden red,
and you must go there now!

Just sleep a little while;
you cannot see or hear.
A fly is crawling round your mouth;
that's just how it is.
Leaves are falling, snow is falling,
twilight grows over your shore.
There is little difference
between that dead man and yourself.

Translated from the Norwegian by Marian de Vooght

DYSENTERIBARAKKEN

Han kommer inn på skjelvende knær,
han står ved ovnen og venter.
Stanken er tykk, og kropp og klær
er våte av ekskrementer.
En balje blir hentet, en sortbrun svamp,
den vasker de mannen med.
Så går han inn til den siste kamp
og den hårde fred.

I tre etasjer er salen full,
til taket full av senger.
En sekk med halm og et teppe av ull

er alt et menneske trenger.
Du hadde så mange behov, min venn,
se her er din suppeskål.
Og dagene, dem du har igjen,
får du ta med tål.

Han ligger og gåper gustengrå,
med jordslåtte knokkelnever.
Da reiser han sig op og vil gå,
og du kan se, at han lever.
Det var vel noget, han vilde ha gjort;
men han sovner, han kan ikke kny.
I lakenet tar de og bærer ham bort
og nu har de plass til en ny.

Så anderledes tar livet slutt,
enn alt hvad du hadde ventet.
Det ligger og lokker til siste minutt
med gaver, du ikke har hentet.
En hage åpner sig underfull,
det leker i gyllen lind;
og eplene er av det røde gull,
og nu skal du gå derinn!

Du må bare sove en liten stund;
du kan ikke se eller høre.
En flue kryper omkring din munn;
det får den heller gjøre.
Der faller løv og der faller sne,
det skumrer over din strand.
Og der er liten forskjell å se
på dig og den døde mann.

ANDRÉ VERDET

This poem was written in Buchenwald in August 1944. Verdet was a French artist and poet, imprisoned there because of his participation in the French Resistance. He published his poems and those by fellow inmates in an anthology in 1946. He died in 2004.

POEM OF THE HOURS

The day departs like some old king
who's lost possession of his crown
to barbarous foreigners. Alone
on exile's road he turns around
just at the corner of a wood
meanwhile his country's frontiers
disintegrate beneath his feet
The day departs like some old king

Night comes, a woman, penniless
poor thing whom Love and Glory once
feted, resplendent in their shine
She buttonholes the passer-by
begs him to let her have some stars
but off he hurries muttering
that madness is peculiar
Night comes, a woman, penniless

The morning's like an orphan child
who keeps on looking for a smile
a game a bird a flower's cry
till Death runs up to tell him this
you're numbered with the restless dead
caught in that narrow ashen void
the dead they still are torturing
The morning's like an orphan child

Translated from the French by Timothy Adès

POÈME DES HEURES

Le jour s'en va comme un vieu roi
Dépossédé de sa couronne
Par de barbares étrangers
Seul sur la route de l'exil
Il se retourne au coin d'un bois
Quand les frontières du pays
Déjà s'effacent sous ses pas
Le jour s'en va come un vieux roi

La nuit s'en vient comme une pauvre
Qu'Amour et Gloire jadis comblèrent
Et réfléchirent dans leurs lustres
Elle interpelle le passant
Et lui mendie quelques étoiles
Mais lui se hâte en murmurant
Que la folie est chose étrange
La nuit s'en vient comme une pauvre

Le matin semble un orphelin
Toujours en quête d'un sourire
D'un jeu d'oiseau d'un cri de fleur
Mais la mort seule accourt lui dire
Qu'il est des morts qui dorment mal
Dans leur étroit néant de cendre
Des morts que l'on torture encore
Le matin semble un orphelin

NELLY SACHS

Sachs was born in Berlin in 1891. Narrowly escaping deportation to a concentration camp, she fled to Sweden, becoming a prolific translator of Swedish poetry. She won the Nobel Prize for literature in 1966. She died in Stockholm in 1970. This is one of her later poems, that imagines the situation of people in a gas chamber.

THEY NO LONGER WEEP AND WAIL...

They no longer weep and wail
when the pain comes
One treads on the wounds of the other
but it's only clouds
they step on now
that drip like ghosts –

Translated from the German by Jean Boase-Beier

SIE SCHREIEN NICHT MEHR...

Sie schreien nicht mehr
wenn es weh tut
Einer steigt auf die Wunden des Andern
aber es sind nur Wolken
auf die sie treten
die tropfen denn geisterhaft –

JAAN KAPLINSKI

Kaplinski was born in 1941 in Tartu. Estonia did not have a large population of Jews, but people were brought in from other countries to be killed at the Kalevi-Liiva site. Kaplinski's Polish-Jewish father was arrested by Soviet troops and died in a Gulag camp in 1945.

THEY ARE STANDING UP TO THEIR KNEES IN BLOOD AND MUD...

They are standing up to their knees in blood and mud,
up to their knees, *not on their knees,*
at the gas chambers, *not gas stoves,*
saying that life is beautiful...
I cannot, I cannot once more...

The world is a dark surface,
a polished surface aslant, aslant,
a world aslant toward Auschwitz,
aslant my town,
my town, my home, my wife and child
high up on the thin edge – below,
only smooth polished wood,
black wood, and high up
you, me, all of us
and looking down one feels
his heart falling, his blood flowing straight down,
down – *no one is strong enough,*
nobody demolished the gas chambers,
nobody made peace:
this all exists from the beginning,
war in peace, peace in war. All in all
how long can we stand here, how long

believing life is beautiful,
that *everyone gets his due*, that *work makes us free*?
Under millions of eyes that are ashes
we are standing on a sleek thin board
above millions of eyes that are ashes.

Only together with them might one be happy,
and they are looking at me with millions of eyes
and my pale blood is flowing straight down
hoping to find a pure hope, a handful of pure land
under the sun's distorting mirror, under this slanting land,
these white clouds and the jubilant endless indifference
of the last skylarks.
My love, I am again falling on my eyes
into the ashes of those I could have been,
on my eyes into their burnt eyes
as if it were not painful enough to be born
on white sheets under a dark light
to become executioner or victim. I know
that everything is
only lightning reflected in dewdrops, suffering
the more distant, the more real, what was forgotten
returns in this way, towers breaking, railways melting,
fishes drowning – my eyes, why
do you not help me – dead,
why do you not help me to live – the Creator
has not yet said his first word? But
has the end not ended, the beginning not begun?
Everything is something else for him
who writes and reads, but no one of us
speaks truth when he says he knows why,
whither, with what, to whom, how long
we are said, written, shaped
to have a meaning. – Even that
is too much for words. PEACE
is too big. In peace
there is room for everything. But how
can I be there together with those that are not,

how can killers be together with the killed
meaning one and the same thing. TOO MUCH
you are to me, world, why
didn't you leave me in your unconscious
flowering clover?

Translated from the Estonian by Jaan Kaplinski & Sam Hamill

NAD SEISAVAD PÕLVINI VERES JA PORIS...

Nad seisavad põlvini veres ja poris
põlvini MITTE PÕLVILI
gaasikambrite MITTE GAASIPLIITIDE ees
ja ütlevad et elu on ilus
mina ei saa mina jälle ei saa

maailm on tume must pind
poleeritud puu kaldu kaldu
maailm kaldu Auschwitzi poole
kaldu minu linn
linn ja kodu naine ja laps
ülal õhukesel serval – all
sile poleeritud puu
must puu ja üleval
sina mina meie üleval
ja alla vaadates tunned
südant langevat verd voolavat püstloodis alla
alla – KEEGI POLE KÜLLALT TUGEV
gaasikambreid pole keegi lammutanud
rahu pole keegi teinud
kõik see on olemas ALGUSEST SAADIK
sõda rahus rahu sõjas kõik kõiges
kaua siis meie püsime siin kaua
uskudes et elu on ilus
et igaüks saab oma et töö teeb vabaks
miljonite silmade all mis on tuhk
seisame meie ahtal libedal laual
miljonite silmade kohal mis on tuhk

ainult nendega koos võiks õnnelik olla
ja nad vaatavad mulle otsa tuhk oma miljoni silmaga
ja mu kaame very voolab püstloodis ära alla
lootes leida puhast lootust peotäit puhast maad
selle päikese kõverpeegli selle viltuse maa
valgete pilvede ja viimaste lõokeste
otsatu juubeldava ükskõiksuse all
armas ma vajun jälle silmili

nende tuhka kes ma võinuksin olla
silmili nende põlenud silmadesse
nagu sündida isegi poleks küllalt raske
valgeil linadel pimeda valguse all
tapetuks või tapjaks MA TEAN
et see on et kõik on
kastepiiskadel peegelduv välk KANNATUS
mida kaugem seda tõelisem unustatu
naaseb nii murduvad tornid sulavad raudteed
uppuvad kalad mu silmad miks
te ei aita mind armas kallis tuhk miks
sa ei aita mind surnud miks
te ei aita mul elada – looja
ei ole öelnud veel esimest sõna VEEL
on olemata lõpp algus tõeks saamata
kõik on midagi muud TEMA JAOKS
kes kirjutab ja loeb aga keegi meist
ei räägi õigust öeldes et ta teab milleks
kuhu millega kellele kui kauaks
oleme meie öeldud kirjutatud voolitud
midagi tähendama – seegi
on sõnades liig RAHU
on liiga suur rahusse
mahub kõik ainult kuidas
saan mina olla seal olematutega koos
kuidas saavad tapjad olla tabetutega koos
tähendades ühte ja sama LIIGA PALJU
on mulle sind maailm miks
sa ei jäta mind oma teadvuseta
õitsemisse ristikhein

SALLY PINKHOF

Pinkhof wrote this poem in Bergen-Belsen, where he died in 1944. He was the brother of the Dutch, later Israeli, author Clara Asscher-Pinkhof.

MY SKINNY LEGS

My skinny legs,
your flesh is gone!
My battered shins,
you look like a messy
but rather substantial
and permanent palette,
a large work of art

in mauve, red and mud,
for the blows and the thuds!
And here, what a hoot,
these loose-fitting tendons
and bones in my foot!
And clusters of veins,
sagging to baggy
and sickly blue stains!
White hide, slack and pleated,
no content, depleted!
To be seated was never
so tough on the thighs!
A push in the side
I can stand with a sigh,
but pavement and stones
I cannot step over –
I'm all skin and bones.

Translated from the Dutch by Marian de Vooght

MIJN MAGERE BENEN

Mijn magere benen,
je vlees is verdwenen!
Gehavende schenen,
je lijkt een onnet
maar fors opgezet
en blijvend palet,
een schilderstuk groot
in paars, bruin en rood,
door schram en door stoot!
Mijn voet met je zotte,
beweeglijke schotten
van pezen en botten!
En aderbossen,
verzakkend in losse
en ziekblauwe trossen!
Wit vel, slap geplooid,
van inhoud berooid!
Het zitten was nooit
zó hard voor de dijen!
Een duwtje bezijen
kan 'k wankel nog lijen,
maar stoepen en stenen
kom 'k nauw overhenen –
mijn magere benen!

UNKNOWN YOUTH [UNBEKANNTER JUGENDLICHER]

This poem was written in the Plötzensee Prison in Berlin in 1942.

DESPAIR

My mother will pass away.
My sweetheart will betray me.
My friends will all forget me.
I'll have nothing more to say
And never find any way
To begin my life again.
I am nineteen. Plus two.
Nineteen out in the world.
Two in this monotony.
These cold, these high
Walls of grey.

Translated from the German by Philip Wilson

VERZWEIFLUNG

Meine Mutter wird mir sterben,
Meine Liebste untreu werden
Meine Freundschaft mich vergessen,
Und ich werde nichts mehr wissen
Nichts mehr sagen können,
Neu das Leben zu beginnen,
Neunzehn zähl ich – und zwei;
Neunzehn draussen in der Weite.
Zwei in diesem Einerlei.
Kalter, grauer
Hoher Mauern.

IRENA BOBOWSKA

Bobowska was born in 1920 in Poznań. She was a poet and an active member of the Polish Resistance, though confined to a wheelchair since childhood. She was imprisoned in 1940 for editing an underground newspaper, and executed in Berlin in 1942.

SO I LEARN LIFE'S GREATEST ART...

So I learn life's greatest art:
Always and everywhere to laugh
And to suffer pain without despair,
And not to mourn for what is gone,
And not to fear what still must come!

I have got to know the taste of hunger
And sleepless nights (once, long ago)
And I know the jab of cold
When you want to roll up in a ball
And I know what it means to shed tears of weakness
Sometimes in the light of day
Sometimes in the dark of night

And I have learned in my thoughts to hurry
Time, that loves to drag remorselessly.

And I know how hard I must fight with myself,
Not to lose heart, not to lose spirit
On this journey that seems without end.

And still I learn life's greatest art
Always and everywhere to laugh
And to suffer pain without despair
Not to mourn for what is gone
And not to fear what still must come.

Someone's fingers stroke across the keys
And the violin's strings are touched by a hand
Some distant tune comes near –
I want to remember but the sounds blur
At night I dream of our piano –

Black and shiny it stands by the wall –
And waits for me when the grey days are past
I will go back to it – when I am free again…
But for now I just dream and compose my rhymes
Sometimes – though rarely – shedding tears
And tell myself fairytales,
And laugh when I dream

I construct a shining, light-filled future
As its basis kindness
And then my cell ceases to be dark
The sun shines gold through the bars –
And in the bright sun's rays
In the glow of true hallucination
The soul bathes as in a stream
And my heart beats more lightly.

Through the stars, the moon, through the rays of the sun
Through everything that glows
I send my greetings home
And my heart full of longing
Through the trees, the bushes, through the breath of the wind
Through everything that blooms and grows
I send my greetings home

And my dreams of spring
Through the fresh green, through the blue of the sky
Over the sparkling play of the rainbow's colours
I send my greetings home
In the sounds of a song of lament.

Translated from the Polish by Jean Boase-Beier, Marian de Vooght & Gunter Spieß

BO JA SIĘ UCZĘ NAJWIĘKSZEJ SZTUKI ŻYCIA...

Bo ja się uczę największej sztuki życia:
Uśmiechać się zawsze i wszędzie
I bez rozpaczy znosić bóle,
I nie żałować tego co przeszło,
I nie bać się tego co będzie!

Poznałam smak głodu
I bezsennych nocy (to było dawno)
I wiem jak kłuje zimno
Gdy w kłębek chciałbyś skulony,
I wiem co znaczy lać łzy niemocy
W niejeden dzień jasny,
Niejedną noc ciemną

I nauczyłam się popędzać myślami
Czas, co bezlitośnie lubi się dłużyć.

I wiem jak ciężko trzeba walczyć z sobą,
Aby nie upaść i nie dać się znużyć
Nie kończącą zda się drogą.

I dalej uczę się najcięższej sztuki życia
Uśmiechać się zawsze i wszędzie
Bez rozpaczy znosić bóle,
Nie żałować tego co przeszło
I nie bać się tego co będzie.

Ktoś po klawiszach palcami wodzi
O struny skrzypiec czyjaś ręka trąca
Jakaś melodia z dala nadchodzi –
Chcę ją spamiętać, lecz tony się mącą –
Śni mi się w nocy nasze pianino –
Czarne i lśniące stoi pod ścianą –
I na mnie czeka, gdy dni szare mina
Wrócę do niego – gdy wolna zostanę…
Na razie śnię tylko I rymy układam
Czasem – choć rzadko – łzy leję
I bajki sobie opowiadam,
I do snów moich się śmieję

Buduję przyszłość promienną, jasną
Podkłady daję z dobroci
I wtedy cela przestaje być ciemną
Przez kraty słońce ją złoci –
A w słonecznej jasnej strudze
W blasku prawdziwych urojeń
Dusza się kąpie jak w strudze
I lżej oddycha serce moje

Przez gwiazdy, księżyc i słońca promienie
Przez wszystkie blaski istniejące

Zasyłam w dom mój pozdrowienia
I moje serce tęskniące
Przez drzewa, krzewy i przez wiatru tchnienie
Przez wszystko co kwitnie i rośnie
Zasyłam w dom mój pozdrowienia

I moje sny o wiośnie
Przez świeżą zieleń, przez błękit nieba
Poprzez gry kolorów tęczowych lśnienie
Zasyłam w dom mój pozdrowienia
W tonach żałobnej piosenki.

DIETRICH BONHOEFFER

Bonhoeffer, a German pastor, was a founding member of the Confessing Church in Nazi Germany. For his open opposition to the persecution of the Jews and the murder of mentally ill and disabled people, he was imprisoned at Tegel prison in Berlin, and executed by hanging at Flossenbürg in 1945.

WHO AM I?

Who am I? Often they say
I step from my cell
in a relaxed and cheerful way,
as a landowner steps from his mansion.
Who am I? Often they say
I chat with my guards
in a free and friendly way,
as though I were the one who gave orders.
Who am I? They also say
I bear these days of pain
in a poised and smiling way,
as one long accustomed to win.

Am I really like this, like the others say?
Or am I just what I know of myself?
Unquiet, longing, sick, like a bird in its cage,
fighting for life-breath, as if someone were squeezing my throat,
hungry for colour, for flowers, for birdsong,
thirsty for kind words, for human contact,
trembling in fury at happenstance, tiniest insults,

buffeted round with waiting for grandiose things,
helplessly fearful for friends in unreachable places,
tired and too empty to pray or to think or to act,
weary and ready to take my leave from it all.

Who am I? This one or that?
Am I one today and tomorrow the other?
Or both at once? Before others a hypocrite,
by myself a weakling, cringing and pitiful?
Or is all that is left of me more like the vanquished army,
fleeing in chaos from the victory already won?

Who am I? Lonely questioning plays its mocking game.
Whoever I am. Lord I am yours. You know my name.

Translated from the German by Jean Boase-Beier

WER BIN ICH?

Wer bin ich? Sie sagen mir oft,
ich träte aus meiner Zelle
gelassen und heiter und fest,
wie ein Gutsherr aus seinem Schloß.
Wer bin ich? Sie sagen mir oft,
ich spräche mit meinen Bewachern
frei und freundlich und klar,
als hätte ich zu gebieten.
Wer bin ich? Sie sagen mir auch,
ich trüge die Tage des Unglücks
gleichmütig, lächelnd und stolz,
wie einer, der Siegen gewohnt ist.

Bin ich das wirklich, was andere von mir sagen?
Oder bin ich nur das, was ich selbst von mir weiß?
Unruhig, sehnsüchtig, krank, wie ein Vogel im Käfig,
ringend nach Lebensatem, als würgte mir einer die Kehle,
hungernd nach Farben, nach Blumen, nach Vogelstimmen,
dürstend nach guten Worten, nach menschlicher Nähe,
zitternd vor Zorn über Willkür und kleinlichste Kränkung,
umgetrieben vom Warten auf große Dinge,
ohnmächtig bangend um Freunde in endloser Ferne,
müde und leer zum Beten, zum Denken, zum Schaffen,
matt und bereit, von allem Abschied zu nehmen?

Wer bin ich? Der oder jener?
Bin ich denn heute dieser und morgen ein andrer?
Bin ich beides zugleich? Vor Menschen ein Heuchler
und vor mir selbst ein verächtlich wehleidiger
    Schwächling?
Oder gleicht, was in mir noch ist, dem geschlagenen Heer,
das in Unordnung weicht vor schon gewonnenem Sieg?

Wer bin ich? Einsames Fragen treibt mit mir Spott.
Wer ich auch bin. Du kennst mich, Dein bin ich, o Gott!

ALFRED SCHMIDT-SAS

A poem written in the Berlin Plötzensee prison; it was published with the note "Mit gefesselten Händen geschrieben", that is "Written with hands bound", composed when Schmidt-Sas had been sentenced to death for producing antifascist material. He was beheaded in 1943.

STRANGE LIGHTNESS OF LIFE SO CLOSE TO DEATH

Nearly nine paces long
is my final whitewashed world
    perhaps nine days left
        then off,
       my head
that now still thinks and speaks and sees and hears.

So near me now the big sleep waits
with its dark wing casting into shade
the luminous blaze of hopes or fears,
to lighten the longest, the blackest
the bitterest moments of human despair.
Strange lightness of life so close to death.

Translated from the German by Jean Boase-Beier

O SELTSAM LICHTES LEBEN DICHT AM TOD

Fast neun Schritte lang
ist meine letzte weißgetünchte Welt
vielleicht neun Tage noch
dann fällt
mein Kopf,
der jetzt noch denkt und spricht und sieht und hört.

So nahe wartet schon der große Schlaf
mit seiner dunklen Schwinge überschattend
die grelle Glut von Wünschen oder Ängsten.
Er sänftigt die längsten, allerbängsten,
die Augenblicke bitt'rer Menschennot.
O seltsam lichtes Leben dicht am Tod.

MELANIA FOGELBAUM

See the note for Fogelbaum's poem 'Spring Evening', p. 54.

THE GUT DIGESTS...

The gut digests emptiness
leeches blind to hunger
daybreak not for us, hunger tears through open eyes
the emptiness of the gut and the bowel's violet flowers
quiver bluely beneath the heart like wild peonies
leeches blind to pain will suck in the warmth within

Translated from the Polish by Jean Boase-Beier with Dieter Beier

TRZEWIE TRAWIĄ...

Trzewie trawią próżnię
ślepe głodu pijawy
świt nie dla nas, przez oczy otwarte głód targnie
próżnię trzewi i jelit fioletowe kwiaty
zadrżą sino pode sercem jak dzikie peonie
ślepe bólu pijawy w ciepło wnętrza się wessą

GERTRUD KOLMAR

Born in Berlin in 1894, Kolmar was a translator and language teacher. She suffered forced labour in an armaments factory, and was transported to Auschwitz in March 1943, but the place and date of her death are not known.

THE ABUSED

All night long the light burns in my cell.
I must not sleep, I stand against the wall;

A guard comes every ten minutes to check.
His shirt is brown. By the wall I stay awake.

The others come back now to play their cruel games
To pass the time, they mock my groans and screams,

They yank and twist my arms and call it sport.
My knees give way… at last then they withdraw.

I see no trees, no sun – is there any such thing?
And are there still fathers whose children love them?

No word, no letter – and I have a wife! –
They said "You're a red; we'll beat you within an inch of your life"

So they whipped my bare body blue with rods of steel…
O God! O God! But no! No, I don't believe,

I never prayed in hospital bed or field,
But only, while my mother watched, at night as a child.

The earth is a prison-grave, the sky an empty blue.
Do you hear, I deny you! But O God… hear me, please do!

You're dead. If you weren't, you would hear my plea.
Jesus suffered for us all; but I suffer just for me.

I stand, collapse. We get only water and dry bread
Hour after hour. How good, oh how good to be dead!

Laid out... locked in a dungeon dark and deep.
No bright lamps. Silence, night, sleep...

Translated from the German by Jean Boase-Beier

DER MISSHANDELTE

In meiner Zelle brennt die ganze Nacht das Licht.
Ich stehe an der Wand und schlafen darf ich nicht;

Denn alle zehn Minuten kommt ein Wärter, mich zu schaun.
Ich wache an der Wand. Sein Hemd ist braun.

Die andern kehren wieder, unterhalten sich
Mit meinem Schrein und Stöhnen, lachen über mich,

Sie recken mir die Arme gewaltsam, nennen's Sport.
Ich breche in die Knie... und endlich gehn sie fort.

Ich seh nicht Bäume, Sonne – ob es die wirklich gibt?
Ob wo ein armes Kind noch seinen Vater liebt?

Kein Zeichen mehr, kein Brief – und ich habe doch eine Frau! –
Sie sagten: "Du bist rot; wir schlagen dich braun und blau."

Sie peitschten mit stählernen Ruten und mein Rumpf war bloß...
O Gott! O Gott! Nein, nein! Ich bin ja glaubenslos,

Ich habe nicht gebetet im Felde, im Lazarett,
Nur abends als kleiner Junge, und die Mutter saß am Bett.

Die Erde ist Kerkergruft, der Himmel ein blaues Loch.
Hörst du, ich leugne dich! Mein Gott... ach, hilf mir doch!

Du bist nicht: wenn du wärst, erbarmtest du dich mein.
Jesus litt für uns alle; ich leide für mich allein.

Ich steh und sinke ein bei Wasser und wenig Brot
Stunden und aber Stunden. Wie gut, wie gut ist der Tod!

Hingelegt... und verschlossen in tiefem, dunklem Schacht.
Keine grelle Lampe. Nur Schlaf. Nur Stille. Nacht...

MIKLÓS RADNÓTI

Radnóti was born in Budapest in 1909. He was made to endure several periods of forced labour, writing this poem, among others, in a camp in Serbia. He was shot in 1944 during a forced march. His body was later found in a ditch and the poems recovered from his pocket.

POSTCARD (4)

I tumbled beside him, his body twisted and then,
like a snapped string, up it sprang again.
Neck shot. "This is how you'll be going too"
I whispered to myself, "just lie easy now"
Patience is blossoming into death.
"Der springt noch auf", rang out above me. Mud
dried on my ear, mingled with blood.

Szentkirályszabadja, 31st Oct. 1944

Translated from the Hungarian by Francis R. Jones

RAZGLEDNICA (4)

Mellézuhantam, átfordult a teste
s feszes volt már, mint húr, ha pattan.
Tarkólövés. – Így végzed hát te is, –
súgtam magamnak, – csak feküdj nyugodtan.
Halált virágzik most a türelem. –
Der springt noch auf, – hangzott fölöttem.
Sárral kevert vér száradt fülemen.

Szentkirályszabadja, 1944. okt 31.

HUGO CLAUS

This is one of the poems writer, artist and film director Claus, who was born in 1929, wrote in response to a series of photographs by Rik Selleslags, taken in Brussels in October, 1943. Claus died in 2008.

EVERY SUMMER REBECCA LIVED AMONG US...

Every summer Rebecca lived among us.
Her wagon stood on the square by the church.

Rebecca read in our palms
the future of our street.
(While her children were stealing
our turnips.)

When the war's summer came
she did not appear,
Rebecca with her oiled hair,
her snowy teeth.

She did not predict her future.
Executed.

Translated from the Dutch by Marian de Vooght

ELKE ZOMER WOONDE REBECCA ONDER ONS...

Elke zomer woonde Rebecca onder ons.
Haar huifkar stond op het plein bij de kerk.

Rebecca las in onze handpalm
de toekomst van onze straat.
(Ondertussen stalen haar kinderen
onze knolrapen.)

Toen de zomer van de oorlog kwam
bleef zij weg,
Rebecca met haar geolied haar,
haar sneeuwgebit.

Haar toekomst heeft zij niet voorspeld.
Terechtgesteld.

ANDRÁS MEZEI

Mezei survived the Holocaust in Budapest, and often wrote in his poems about the mass murder of Jews, Roma and other people in Hungary during 1944 and early 1945. He died in 2008.

GUSTAV!

Feinstein, a Jew from Memel,
recognized his neighbour
in the execution squad.
And he cried out to him:
Gustav! aim
straight between the eyes!

Translated from the Hungarian by Thomas Ország-Land

TANÚVALLOMÁS II

Feinstein a memmeli zsidó
felismerte lakószomszédját
a kivégzőosztagban.
Oda is kiáltott neki:
Gusztáv!
Pontosan célozz!

MATILDA OLKINAITĖ

See the note preceding Olkinaitė's poem 'During the Gnosiology Lesson', p. 29. The following poem is dated 27 March 1940.

ALL THE SKIFFS HAVE FOUNDERED

All the skiffs have foundered
And mine will sink as well.
Death is wading
Through troubled waters.

And Death bade me
Sing my final hymn.
And Death bade me
Dance my final dance.

And so I sing my hymn
To the seagulls and the swells.
The azure heavens listen,
And I sing to them too.

And the sea carries my skiff
Through a window,
Carries me away to sleep,
And will pull me under.

Tonight Death wanders
Through restless waters.
The sun has sunk already
And my skiff will sink as well.

Translated from the Lithuanian by Laima Vincė

VISŲ LAIVAS NUSKENDO...

Visų laivas nuskendo...
Ir mano laivas skęs.
Mirtis šia naktį brenda
Po neramias mares.

Ir paskutinę giesmę
Man liepė padainuot,
Ir paskutinį šokį
Ji liepė man pašokt.

Ir aš dainuoju giesmę
Žuvėdroms ir bangoms.
Padangės melsvos klausos,
Ir aš dainuoju joms.

Ir neša mano laivą
Įėjusi langą.
Nuneš į miega laivą
Ir nuskandins mane...

Mirtis šią naktį braido,
Po neramias mares.
Jau saulė nusileido,
Ir mano laivas skęs.

YUKIKO SUGIHARA

The four tanka that follow originally appeared in the book Visas for Life *by Yukiko Sugihara, the wife of Chiune Sugihara, who was consul in Kaunas, Lithuania. Chiune issued numerous transit visas for people fleeing the Nazis, so they were able to escape via Japan.*

On the park railing,
　　　　　　in blunt German:
　　　　　　　　　　"No Jews Allowed".

Fretting on visa decisions,
　　　　　　restless –
　　　　　　　　I hear my husband's bed creak.

In the flock of people awaiting visas,
　　　　　　　an infant, his face dirty,
　　　　　　　　　　kneads his father's hand.

The train pulls out,
　　　　　　pressed into a grasping hand –
　　　　　　　　　　the fateful visa.

Translated from the Japanese by James Hadley & Nell Regan

　　　かたきドイツ語にて公園の柵に記しあり「ユダヤ人入るを禁ず」

　　　ビザ交付の決断に迷ひ眠れざる夫のベッドの軋むを聞けり

　　　ビザを待つ人群に父親の手を握る幼な子はいたく顔汚れをり

　　　走り出づる列車の窓に縋りくる手に渡さるる命のビザは

MIKLÓS RADNÓTI

See the note on Radnóti before the poem 'Postcard (4)', on p. 96. It was during a forced march like the one described here that Radnóti was shot.

FORCED MARCH

It's a fool who, fallen to earth,   gets up and trudges on,
flexes his ankle and knee,   a single walking pain,
but still, as if lifted by wings,   sets off again on his way,
and ignores the ditch's call   nor even dares to wait
and if you ask, why not?   who might just find the breath
to say there's a lady waiting   and a wiser, finer death.
But the poor fellow's a fool: back there, since time out of mind,
swirling over each house   there's only the scorched wind.
The plum tree is shattered,   the house wall is felled
and all those homely nights   are matted thick with dread.
If only I could believe   that everything still worthwhile
were not just stored in my heart,   and homecoming might be real;
if the bees of peace were humming   now, like then, out loud
while the plum jam stood cooling   in the old veranda's shade,
if the late summer's silence   still basked on the drowsy garden
and, swinging nude in the leaves,   the fruit were starting to ripen,
if Fanny were still waiting   blonde by the reddening hedge
and the slow forenoon still writing   the shadow's slow edge –
yes, it might still be!   The moon today's so round!
Don't leave – just give me a shout   and I'll get up, my friend!

Bor, 15 September 1944

Translated from the Hungarian by Francis R. Jones

ERŐLTETETT MENET

Bolond, ki földre rogyván   fölkél és újra lépked,
s vándorló fájdalomként   mozdít bokát és térdet,
de mégis útnak indul,   mint akit szárny emel,
s hiába hívja árok,   maradni úgyse mer,
s ha kérdezed, miért nem?   még visszaszól talán,
hogy várja őt az asszony   s egy bölcsebb, szép halál.
Pedig bolond a jámbor,   mert ott az otthonok
fölött régóta már csak   a perzselt szél forog,
hanyattfeküdt a házfal,   eltört a szilvafa,

és félelemtől bolyhos   a honni éjszaka.
Ó, hogyha hinni tudnám: nemcsak szivemben hordom
mindazt, mit érdemes még,   s van visszatérni otthon;
ha volna még! s mint egykor   a régi hűs verandán
a béke méhe zöngne,   míg hűl a szilvalekvár,
s nyárvégi csönd napozna   az álmos kerteken,
a lomb között gyümölcsök   ringnának meztelen,
és Fanni várna szőkén   a rőt sövény előtt,
s árnyékot írna lassan   a lassú délelőtt, –
de hisz lehet talán még!   a hold ma oly kerek!
Ne menj tovább, barátom,   kiálts rám! s fölkelek!

Bor, 1944. szept. 15

STANISLAV SMELYANSKY

Smelyansky, a former television presenter, was born in Moscow in 1979. His grandmother's relatives suffered greatly in the Holocaust. He is currently working on a rap music album with Holocaust-related lyrics, and his poems about the Holocaust featured in his 2013 novel Flying over Eternity.

DANCING GYPSY

Ai, na-ne-nè, ne-vài – don't kill me!
Ai, na-ne-vài – don't shoot me!
Not a hooligan, not a thief –
I am just a gypsy, a dancing gypsy
My tambourine is all my wealth.
Ai, my soldier, put away your gun.
Let me dance for you – ài, na-ne-nè!
Hey, don't shoot…

Translated from the Russian by Veronika Krasnova

ТАНЦУЮЩИЙ ЦЫГАН

Ай, на-нэ-нэ. Нэ-вай, ай, на-нэ-вай!
Не убивай меня, не убивай.
Не конокрад я и не хулиган.
А я цыган, танцующий цыган.
Мой звонкий бубен – все, чем я богат!
Ай, отведи, солдатик автомат!
Ай, на-нэ-нэ, станцую я давай!
Не убивай меня…

FANIA ŻORNE

Poem written on 8 September, 1942, as an appeal to German mothers, when Jewish children in the Ukrainian-Polish town of Radziwiłłów were rounded up and murdered. The German title given to the Polish poem has the singular form of "mother", but the poem makes it clear that it is used collectively.

OH DEUTSCHE MÜTTER

Oh deutsche Mütter, who so love your children
Never deny them Brot, give them butter
And fill their bellies
While our own perish with not a crust of bread
Perish with longing and die
Thrown around in this great wide world
In the places of hurt and despair.
But if all that you loved was taken away
Through swindle and murder
Your children's golden heads
As though we lived among the Tatar's hordes
If only you heard the cries of the babies
The laments, if you saw the masses of corpses
And you felt the pain and the grief of the mothers
Torn from their children forever.
Somewhere in a camp
With toil and bitter longing
Lost in those places of hurt and despair.
Oh deutsche Mütter – you of no conscience
Your God is Luther
And your heart is stone.

Translated from the Polish by Jean Boase-Beier & Marian de Vooght, with Dieter Beier

O DEUTSCHE MUTTER

O Deutsche Mutter co dzieci swe tak kochacie
I chleb nie postny, lecz z butter
W brzuszki im napychacie
Podczas gdy nasze giną bez kawałka chleba
Giną i mrą z tęsknoty
Rozrzucone po całym świecie
Na placówkach nędzy i zgryzoty.
A gdyby wam zabrano to co kochacie

Na targi i mordy
Te złote główki dziecięce
Że zda się tatarskich hord wróciły czasy
Gdyby wam danym było te krzyki niemowlęce
I jęki, a po tym widzieć trupków masy
A później doznać bólu i mąk tych matek
Co zostały oderwane od swych dziatek.
By gdzieś po lagrach
Z wysiłków i żrącej tęsknoty
Zginąć na placówkach nędzy i zgryzoty.
O deutsche Mutter – wy bez sumienia
Bo Bóg wam Luter
A serce z kamienia.

TAKIS VARVITSIOTIS

Varvitsiotis was born in 1916 in Thessaloniki. He published Winter Solstice – Chronicle of the Occupation *in 1948. He was one of the few non-Jewish Greek writers who early on acknowledged the terrible fate of the Thessaloniki Jews. He died in 2011.*

IN CLOSED TRAINS

They transport phantoms
Garlands that loathe
The laments of tortuous weddings
Apocalyptic exodus
"You are our brothers"
They cry from the trains
Our lamp is glowing
The darkness won't be able
To penetrate our flesh.

Translated from the Greek by David Connolly

ΣΕ ΚΛΕΙΣΤΑ ΤΡΑΪΝΑ

Μεταφέρουν φαντάσματα
Στεφάνια που αποστρέφονται
Τους θρήνους των μαρτυρικών γάμων
Έξοδος αποκαλυπτική
«Είστε αδερφοί μας»
Φωνάζουν από τα τραίνα
Το λυχνάρι μας είναι ρόδινο
Δε θα μπορέσει το σκοτάδι
Να διαπεράσει τη σάρκα μας.

III
LIFE AFTERWARDS

TUVIA RUEBNER

Ruebner was born in 1924 in Bratislava, Czechoslovakia, into a German-speaking Jewish family. He was allowed to emigrate on his own to Palestine in 1941, but both of his parents, as well as his sister, were murdered in Auschwitz. Ruebner's poetry in Hebrew was first published in 1957.

TESTIMONY

I exist in order to say

this house is not a house,
place of confiscations, parched rock, fear
there by the central square, did I say central square?
Paved wilderness.

I exist in order to say,

this road is not a road,
clung to by its travellers, ascending on dream's rust
from the forest, the sand mountain where
I walk, there, who is walking? There where I used to
walk, a child in the sun
of cessation, with outstretched arms, searching
and searching for my father's face my mother's

I exist in order to say

these are the crossbeams and the chronicles
of my parents, coal,
ash, wind
of my sister in my hair blowing
back and back, a night wind

in my day I exist in order to say
to their nighttime voices *yes, yes* to their weeping, *yes*
to the lost in their house of abeyance, to the falling from its
    wall's shadows
on the fear in my voice saying *yes*
in the emptiness.

Translated from the Hebrew by Rachel Tzvia Back

תְּעוּדָה

אֲנִי קַיָּם כְּדֵי לוֹמַר
בַּיִת זֶה לֹא בַּיִת,
מִשְׁטַח חֲרָמִים, צְחִיחַ סֶלַע, פַּחַד
שָׁם לְיַד הַכְּכָה, אָמַרְתִּי כְּכָר?
צִיָּה מְרֻצֶּפֶת.

אֲנִי קַיָּם כְּדֵי לוֹמַר

דֶּרֶךְ זוֹ לֹא דֶּרֶךְ,
יִלְפְּתוּ אָרְחוֹתֶיהָ, יַעֲלוּ בַּחֲלֻדַּת חֲלוֹם
מִן הַיַּעַר, הַר הַחוֹל
אֲנִי הוֹלֵךְ, שָׁם, מִי הוֹלֵךְ? שֶׁהָיִיתִי
הוֹלֵךְ בְּשַׁעֲלִי יֵלֵךְ, בְּשֶׁמֶשׁ
חֶדָּלוֹן, בִּפְשָׁט יָדַיִם, שׁוֹאֵל,
הוֹלֵךְ שׁוֹאֵל פְּנֵי אָבִי וְאִמִּי

אֲנִי קַיָּם כְּדֵי לוֹמַר

קוֹרוֹת אֲבוֹתַי, פֶּחָם,
אֵפֶר, רוּחַ
אֲחוֹתִי בְּשַׂעֲרִי הַנּוֹשֵׁב
אָחוֹר, אָחוֹר, רוּחַ לֵילִית

בְּיוֹמִי אֲנִי קַיָּם כְּדֵי לוֹמַר
לְקוֹלָם הַלֵּילִי כֵּן, כֵּן לְבִכְיָם, כֵּן
לָאוֹבֵד בְּבֵית אֵינוּתָם, לַנּוֹפֵל מִצֵּל קִירוֹתָיו
עַל פַּחַד קוֹלִי לוֹמַר כֵּן
בַּשֶּׁטַח הָרֵיק.

ALEJANDRA PIZARNIK

Pizarnik's parents were Russian Jews who had fled to Argentina from Europe in the 1930s to escape anti-semitism. She was born in Buenos Aires in 1936 and committed suicide in 1972, a few years after her father's death. The date for the poem is 23 November 1971.

POEM FOR THE FATHER

And it was then
that with his tongue dead and cold in his mouth
he sang the song they wouldn't let him sing
in this world of obscene gardens and shadows
that came untimely to remind him

of songs from his years as a young man
when he couldn't sing the song he wanted to sing
the song they wouldn't let him sing
except through his absent blue eyes
his absent mouth
his absent voice.
Then, from absence's highest tower
his song resonated in the opacity of what's hidden
in the silent expanse
full of restless hollows like the words I write.

Translated from the Spanish by Cecilia Rossi

POEMA PARA EL PADRE

Y fue entonces
que con la lengua muerta y fría en la boca
cantó la canción que no le dejaron cantar
en este mundo de jardines obscenos y de sombras
que venían a deshora a recordarle
cantos de su tiempo de muchacho
en el que no podía cantar la canción que quería cantar
la canción que no le dejaron cantar
sino a través de sus ojos azules ausentes
de su boca ausente
de su voz ausente.
Entonces, desde la torre más alta de ausencia
su canto resonó en la opacidad de lo ocultado
en la extensión silenciosa
llena de oquedades movedizas como las palabras que escribo.

PAUL CELAN

*Celan was born in Czernowitz, Romania, in 1920. In June 1942
Celan arrived home to find his parents gone. They had been taken to a
concentration camp in Ukraine, where his father died and his mother was
shot. Celan drowned himself in the Seine in 1970.*

ASPEN TREE, YOUR LEAVES GLANCE WHITE INTO DARKNESS...

Aspen tree, your leaves glance white into darkness.
My mother's hair did not turn white.

Dandelion, so green is the Ukraine.
My golden-haired mother did not come home.

Rain-cloud, do you edge towards the well?
My quiet mother weeps for us all.

Round star, you loop the golden loop.
My mother's heart was torn by lead.

Oaken door, who pulled you off your hinges?
My gentle mother can not come back.

Translated from the German by Jean Boase-Beier

ESPENBAUM, DEIN LAUB BLICKT WEISS INS DUNKEL...

Espenbaum, dein Laub blickt weiß ins Dunkel.
Meiner Mutter Haar ward nimmer weiß.

Löwenzahn, so grün ist die Ukraine.
Meine blonde Mutter kam nicht heim.

Regenwolke, säumst du an den Brunnen?
Meine leise Mutter weint für alle.

Runder Stern, du schlingst die goldne Schleife.
Meiner Mutter Herz ward wund von Blei.

Eichne Tür, wer hob dich aus den Angeln?
Meine sanfte Mutter kann nicht kommen.

NELO RISI

Risi, born in 1920, was an Italian filmmaker and poet. He deserted from the Italian army and fled to Switzerland in the Second World War. He died in 2015.

CELAN

All this polyglot had to do
was to choose
a language in which to write
the work of a life

He chose one of undoing
a word of stone
absolute poetry
to speak for the silenced millions

Translated from the Italian by Peter Ualrig Kennedy

CELAN

Non aveva che da scegliere
lui il poliglotta
in quale lingua scrivere
l'opera di una vita

Ha scelto quella da annullare
una parola una pietra
poesia assoluta
e che comunica per i milioni che tacciono

GEORGE GÖMÖRI

Gömöri was born in Budapest in 1934, and left Hungary in 1956. He lives in England, where he taught literature at Cambridge University. In this poem, the Piave front is the Italian front on the river Piave during World War I.

MY GRANDFATHER'S JOURNEYS

My grandfather never flew on an aeroplane
and went abroad only once, as a young man,
when as he put it 'they shot my horse from under me
three times out there on the Piave front'
All he really knew about was horses,
buying and selling them I was always a little
afraid of them but still went with him
whenever he went to market His old man's
moustache, fit for a sergeant, suited him
and there was in his bearing something of the Hussar
He could never have imagined the days long train journey
which was to take him, now a sick old man,
across the border for the second time
to a death in this case absolutely certain

Translated from the Hungarian by Clive Wilmer & George Gömöri

NAGYAPÁM UTAZÁSAI

Nagyapám sohasem ült repülőgépen
külföldön csak egyszer járt fiatalon amikor
saját szavaival: „háromszor lőtték ki
alólam a lovat a Piavén"
Igazából csak a lovakhoz értett
azokat adta-vette Én mindig kicsit
féltem a lovaktól de azért vele mentem
hogyha a vásártéren éppen dolga volt
A nagyapai bajusz őrmesterhez illett
és volt valami huszáros a tartásában is
Nem tudta volna elképzelni öregen betegen
azt a napokig tartó vonatutat
amelyik másodízben határon túlra
most már biztos halálba vitte

CHAWWA WIJNBERG

Wijnberg, born in 1942 in Dordrecht, is a Dutch poet, writer and artist. Wijnberg's mother lost most of her family in the Holocaust, but she herself was able to hide with her baby daughter. Her husband, the poet's father, was executed by the Nazis because he participated in the Dutch armed resistance.

ON MUMMY'S LAP

I pointed
with my little finger
child in white
still white
Elleke
that is your cousin Elleke
answered mummy
taken away too
and she closed the album
shut

is
is your cousin
is your cousin Elleke
nothing is
the smoke
from her nervous cigarette
was – a more honest answer

Translated from the Dutch by Marian de Vooght

OP SCHOOT

Ik wees aan
met een klein vingertje
kind in wit
nog wit
Elleke
dat is je nichtje Elleke
antwoordde mama
ook weggehaald
en ze sloot het album
dicht

is
is je nichtje
is je nichtje Elleke
niets is
de rook
uit haar nerveuze sigaret
was – een eerlijker antwoord

JACQUES PRESSER

*Presser published this poem under the pseudonym of J. van Wageningen
in 1956. 25 March 1943 is the day that Presser's wife, Debora Appel, was
taken to the transit camp Westerbork. She was murdered in Sobibor.*

NOCTURNE

25 March 1943

'Asphodel' they call these fields.
Walk here with caution, watch where you tread.
Out of the forest a shade steals
Across the grass towards the ford

And hides beneath a horizon,
One mist further than the pain
In which your heart could not yet live,
But only wait. In vain, in vain.

Arrange these death flowers in a bunch
For the ashless urn, where the heart falls dumb.
And creep into an empty trench
Till Judgement Day. That doesn't come.

Translated from the Dutch by Donald Gardner

NOCTURNE

25 maart 1943

Die weide noem: asphodelos.
Ga zéér behoedzaam, demp uw tred.
Een schim glipt uit de rand van 't bos
Het weivlak over naar het wed

En duikt onder een horizon,
Eén nevel verder dan 't verdriet,
Waarin uw hart niet leven kon,
Slechts wachten. En om niet, om niet.

Nu schik die doodsbloem tot een tuil
Voor d'asloze urn, waar 't hart verstomt.
En kruip zelf in een lege kuil
Tot d'Oordeelsdag. Die óók niet komt.

TAL NITZAN

A poet, writer, editor and translator of Hispanic literature into Hebrew, Nitzan currently lives in Tel Aviv. Etty Hillesum was murdered in Auschwitz. An Interrupted Life, *Hillesum's diaries of 1941-1943 and* Letters from Westerbork, *written in Dutch, were translated into numerous languages.*

I REMEMBER ETTY HILLESUM

Did she still whisper
"Why anticipate trouble"
when transported from Westerbork
to Auschwitz in Wagon Number 12,
"They should be exterminated like fleas,
those petty fears of the future"
as her future rushed towards her
to exterminate her?
Maybe I should pause, retreat
or at least recite
"Why anticipate joy?"
as I hurry past the yellow squares of life
that once were far and sealed
and tonight open towards me
to let me in and out as I wish
while a silly hope for happiness
sways like a jug, too large,
on my head

Translated from the Hebrew by Tal Nitzan & Vivian Eden

אֲנִי נִזְכֶּרֶת בָּאֵתִי הַיְלָסִּים בִּרְחוֹב יְהוֹשֻׁעַ בֶּן-נוּן

הַאִם עוֹד לַחֲשָׁה
«דַּיּוֹ לְיוֹם צָרָתוֹ»
כְּשֶׁיָּצְאָה מִמֶּטְרֶבְּרוּק בְּקָרוֹן מִסְפָּר 21,
«יֵשׁ לְהַדְבִּיר אוֹתָן כְּמוֹ פַּרְעוֹשִׁים
אֶת הַדְּאָגוֹת הַקְּטַנוֹת לֶעָתִיד»
כְּשֶׁאֶץ אֵלֶיהָ הֶעָתִיד לְהַדְבִּירָהּ?
אוּלַי מוּטָב לִי לַעֲצֹר, לָסֶגֶת
אוֹ לִפְתֹּחַ לְשִׁנָּן
«דַּיּוֹ לְיוֹם שִׂמְחָתוֹ»
מוּל רְבוּעֵי הַחַיִּים הַצְּהֻבִּים
שֶׁפַּעַם רָחֲקוּ וְנֶאֶטְמוּ
וְהַלַּיְלָה הֵם נִפְתָּחִים לְפָנַי
שֶׁאָבוֹא וְאֵצֵא מֵהֶם כִּרְצוֹנִי
וְצִפִּיָּה נִבְעֶרֶת לְאֹשֶׁר מִתְנַדְנֶדֶת
כְּמוֹ כַּד גָּדוֹל מִדַּי
עַל רֹאשִׁי

IBOJA WANDALL-HOLM

See information on the poet preceding her poem 'Field Work in Auschwitz', p. 62.

DREAD

I have a number on my arm
I would have forgotten about it
a long time ago
if it were not
twenty years of age
like a small child
– afraid of the dark

Translated from the Danish by Marian de Vooght

ANGST

Jer har et nummer på armen
Jeg ville ha glemt det
for længe siden
hvis det ikke
tyve år gammelt
var som et lille barn
– bange for mørke

FABIO PUSTERLA

Pusterla is a Swiss poet, teacher and translator. Anna Brichtová was born in Prague in 1930, deported to Terezín in 1942 and murdered in Auschwitz in May 1944.

NIGHT VISITATION

You are dreaming of
cratacians, arm-tuggers, the snuffle-dragon.
Who knows what Anna Brichtová dreamed of, who tonight
comes to meet us with her mosaic
of coloured drawings: her house
with the red roof, the trees
in the green meadow, the sky: and outside a lager.
This is the real gift
I've brought back from Prague without telling you.
She was with me on the train, the morning
I thought I was in hell: Stuttgart,
or somewhere down from there, in a thrum
of people who work at God knows what
for God knows whom, just work, striking keys,
sending messages to strangers through thin air.
Just eyes and fingers,
one day after another, the endless
even flow of time, that belongs
for ever to others,
to other than themselves, and the fear, the hatred
of outcast for outcast, this rabble
of lost souls, modern-day slaves. The Great
Beer Drinker, Mrs Blankety-Blank,
the Megatron: my travelling companions.

Who knows what Anna Brichtová dreamed of,
and what dreams you are dreaming, and how you children
see the world. Will you find,
among your games, the game that can save us?

We all hope so
watching you sleep.

Translated from the Italian by Simon Knight

VISITA NOTTURNA

Stai sognando
cratassi, tirabraccia, il drago soffia-naso.
Chissà cosa sognava Anna Brichtova, che stanotte
viene a trovarci con il suo mosaico
di carte colorate: la sua casa
col tetto rosso, gli alberi
nel prato verde, il cielo: e fuori un lager.
Questo è il vero regalo
che ho portato da Praga senza dirtelo.
Era con me sul treno, la mattina
che ho creduto di vivere all'inferno: Stoccarda,
o giù di lì, dentro un ronzare
di gente che lavora a non sa cosa
o per chi, ma lavora, preme tasti,
invia messaggi a ignoti dentro l'aria.
Solo occhi e dita, solo
un giorno dopo l'altro, smisurato
trascorrere di un tempo che non varia, che appartiene
per sempre ad altri,
ad altro che a sé stessi, e la paura, l'odio
del paria contro il paria, questa rissa
d'anime perse, nuovi schiavi. Il Grande
Bevitore di Birra, la Donna Occhi nel Vuoto,
Mazinga, i miei compagni di viaggio.
Chissà come sognava Anna Brichtova,
a cosa sogni tu, e come vedete
il mondo voi bambini. Lo troverete,
fra i vostri giochi, il gioco che ci salvi?
Noi tutti lo speriamo
guardandovi dormire.

GUNVOR HOFMO

Hofmo was born in Oslo in 1921. She became very close to Ruth Maier, a refugee from Germany who came to Norway in 1939. In November 1942, Ruth Maier was deported to Auschwitz, where she was sent to the gas chamber immediately.

ENCOUNTER

On such a rainy night
you know it's her,
your Jewish friend they murdered,
whose body they let burn
together with a thousand others.

The smell rises acrid as the tide is falling.
The birds are whining quietly.
Someone's laughing in the distant twilight…
The voices sound so mild,
as if they are holding night inside.

You just know that she is here
and see her without seeing
and recognise the brown-eyed look
resting coldly like snow
over your despairing sorrow.

And your urge to scream,
rage, weep and pray,
just like a little child
tries to get its way,
everything you were hiding in pain,
melts away underneath.

You hear that quiet voice
just like you used to hear it,
questioning without complaining,
subdued and strangely sad:
Warum sollen wir nicht leiden
wenn so viel Leid ist?

Translated from the Norwegian by Marian de Vooght

MØTE

Slik en regnvåt kveldstund
kjenner du det er henne,
en jødisk venninne de drepte,
hun hvis lik de lot brenne
sammen med tusen andres.

Ram stiger lukten fra fjæren.
Fuglene klynker alt stille.
Noen ler fjernt gjennom skumring...
Stemmene klinger så milde
som de har natt i seg.

Du vet bare at hun er her
og ser henne uten å se
og kjenner det brune blikket
legge seg kjølig som sne
over din rådløse sorg.

Og din trang til å skrike,
rase, gråte og be,
slikt som en liten unge
får viljen sin gjennom ved,
alt som du smertelig gjemte,
smelter vekk under det.

Du hører den myke stemmen
slik du hørte den sist,
spørrende uten klage,
dempet og underlig trist:
Warum sollen wir nicht leiden
wenn so viel Leid ist?

ANDRÉ SARCQ

Sarcq is a playwright and poet who lives in Paris. In the 1980s, Pierre Seel was the first survivor in France to speak about his persecution by the Nazis because he was gay. He was sent to the concentration camp Schirmeck, where he was forced to watch as his lover, Jo, was killed by dogs. Both Pierre and Jo were 18 years old.

TO THE TWICE-MURDERED MEN (THE RAG)

For Jo and for Pierre Seel

For all homosexual men
murdered by the Nazis,
both inside and outside of the camps

> *Pray, Lord,*
> *pray to us,*
> *we are near.*
> PAUL CELAN, 'Tenebrae', *Sprachgitter* (Speech-Grid)

> *A Nothing*
> *were we, are we, shall*
> *we remain, flowering:*
> *the Nothing-, the*
> *No-one-Rose.*
> PAUL CELAN, 'Psalm', *Die Niemandsrose* (No-one-Rose)

If a man also lie with mankind, as he lieth with a woman, both of them have committed an abomination: they shall surely be put to death; their blood shall be upon them.
> LEVITICUS 20: 13.

And stop praying to us
God
stop praying to us

Stop addressing us with your autistic
prayer
because we have sunk into
non-existence
enclosed in the negative
non-
of noun
of shroud
and of memory

Our mode is not one
of being
has no being

Our mode
is the perpetual apnoea
of a rock face of
petrified tears
the perpetual apnoea
of a burning mass of muffled basalt
the tombeau apnoea of the scream
that never escaped

never

Stop praying to us

Because your prayer is all
we've got to deal with
Because your Love
leaves us cold

Yes we are here
mass of outcasts from the memory of the just
alien snow beneath the snow of the Jews
black snow
black snow blackened by the ashes
of shame
snow stained
with the shot of offence

We are here
not taking up any space
not being worth anything in any space
beneath the venerable snow of the Jews
the Gypsies and the Fragile-Minded
the snow that fell praying
or not
the snow fused with fine crystals of charcoal
flesh

the slow and infinitely heavy snow
the slow and eternally heavy snow
the slow snow shot dead
in the black-German sod

Stop praying to us
Stop praying to us enough is enough

Lovers of the men erased
from the long lists of martyrs
we flounder in a non-existence
hidden under the waves of our blood

Our blood rises to our ankles

Endless silent squad
stifled to annihilation
we move to the point without name
that will eliminate all names

And the tatter
not the flower
the scrap not the rose
the rag
the soiled rag
the rag of a pool of souls
the agonised rag of no-one and
nothing
the rag crowns our floundering

Our future among mankind
will be not to have been

Our future among mankind is the
unspeaking
of the higher layer of the Jews and the Gypsies
(flowering in the warmth between our shadows
Oh forbidden memory
of the gentle Fragile-Minded folk)

our negative non-
future
lies in our absence of sons
and the survivors' shame
lies in the silence they guard
like a cold sheath covering the noise
about our triangle of blood

We were the living ones of the Book
we were the reviled ones of the Book where the stigma
took root
reviled branch were
crushed
with our hard root
same flesh same meat
but in the ashes and in the
snow
the crystals were well sorted
the separation
restored
honour
biblically counted

Which sons take up which word
take the path of a language
grafted
into our empty mouth

Which sons and if not
which trace of our bones
which uncountable mark on our ruined
bodies

Footnote to the mass grave radiating an insatiable
silence

Lovers of men
lovers of men stand up

And perhaps God
will pray to us

God happy with the order
ruling in families
perhaps his Trinity is inclined towards us

Three times denied we deny him
We deny his prayer
we deny and denounce it interred in
Schirmeck

Here

Schirmeck

Alsace

Here

eponymous abattoir

Here

forever

a child

of eighteen

howling

his head

in a zinc bucket

howling

naked

in the middle of a square of slaves

A mad

dog

has torn off

his genitals

Others

tear at him

from all sides

The child

howling

and his lover

among the slaves

pleading

pleading destroyed

for him to die

and taking him away

in death

far away from the jeers

of the torturers

Here

Schirmeck

Forever

Here

forever

Jo.

Translated from the French by Marian de Vooght & Jean Boase-Beier

AUX HOMMES TUÉS DEUX FOIS
(LA GUENILLE)

A Jo et à Pierre Seel

Aux homosexuels
massacrés par les nazis,
dans et hors des camps.

> *Prie, Seigneur,*
> *prie-nous,*
> *nous sommes proches.*
>   PAUL CELAN, ‹Tenebrae› (Grille de parole).

> *Un rien*
> *nous étions, nous sommes, nous*
> *resterons, en fleur:*
> *la rose de rien, de*
> *personne.*
>   PAUL CELAN, ‹Psaume› *La rose de personne*

> *Quand un homme couche avec un homme comme on*
> *couche avec une femme, ce qu'ils ont fait tous deux est une*
> *abomination ; ils seront mis à mort, leur sang retombe sur eux.*
>   LÉVITIQUE, XX, 13.

Et ne nous prie plus
Dieu
ne nous prie plus

Ne tourne plus vers nous ta prière
autistique
car nous sommes coulés dans le
non
encastrés dans l'a
privatif
de nom
de linceul
et de mémoire

Notre mode n'est pas
d'être
n'a pas d'être

Notre mode
est l'apnée perpétuelle
d'une falaise de larmes

pétrifiées
l'apnée perpétuelle
d'un bloc brûlant de basalte sans bouche
l'apnée tombeau du cri
jamais jailli

jamais

Ne nous prie plus

Car nous n'avons que faire
de ta prière
car ton Amour
nous indiffère

Oui nous sommes là
bloc de bannis de la mémoire des justes
neige étrangère sous la neige des Juifs
neige noire
noire neige noircie des cendres
de la honte
neige salie
de la grenaille de l'offense

Nous sommes là
qui n'occupons nul espace
ne pesons rien dans nul espace
sous la neige vénérable des Juifs
des Tziganes et des Débiles
la neige retombée priante
ou non
la neige mêlée de fins cristaux de chair-
charbon
la neige lente et lourde infiniment
la neige lente et lourde éternellement
la neige lente fusillée
aux champs de tourbe noire-allemande

Ne nous prie plus
Ne nous prie plus c'en est assez

Amants des hommes effacés
des longs registres du martyre
nous piétinons dans un non-être
couvert des flots de notre sang

Notre sang monte à nos chevilles

Interminable troupe muette
pressée jusqu'à la résorption
nous migrons vers le point sans nom
qui abolira tous les noms

Et le chiffon
non la fleur
le lambeau non la rose
la guenille
la guenille souillée
la guenille d'une flaque d'âmes
la guenille agonie de personne et de
rien
la guenille couronne notre piétinement

Notre avenir parmi les hommes
est de n'être pas advenus

Notre avenir parmi les hommes est le
mutisme
de la couche supérieure des Juifs et des Tziganes
(fleuris au chaud entre nos ombres
O mémoire abolie
du tendre peuple des Débiles)
notre avenir a
privatif
est dans notre absence de fils
et la honte des survivants
est dans le silence qu'on garde
comme un fourreau froid au vacarme
sur notre triangle de sang

Nous fûmes les vivants du Livre
nous fûmes les honnis du Livre où racine
la flétrissure
rameau honni fûmes
broyés
avec notre racine dure
même chair et même hachis
mais dans la cendre et dans la
neige
les cristaux furent bien triés
la séparation
restaurée
l'honneur
bibliquement compté

Quels fils prendront quelle parole
prendront la sente d'une langue
greffée
dans notre bouche vide

Quels fils et sinon
quelle trace de notre ossuaire
quelle empreinte innombrable à nos corps
dévastés

Note charnier rayonne d'un silence
insatiable

Amants des hommes
amants des hommes levez-vous

Et Dieu peut-être
nous prie

Dieu heureux de l'ordre
qui règne dans les familles
peut-être vers nous penche sa Trinité

Trois fois niés nous le nions
Nous nions sa prière
Nous la nions et renions enrochés dans
Schirmeck

Ici

Schirmeck

Alsace

Ici

abattoir éponyme

Ici

éternellement

un enfant

de dix-huit ans

hurle

la tête

dans un seau de fer-blanc

hurle

nu

au centre d'un carré d'esclaves

Un chien

fou

lui a arraché

le sexe

D'autres

le déchirent

de tous côtés

L'enfant

hurle

et son amant

parmi les esclaves

supplie

détruit supplie

qu'il meure

et l'emporte

en sa mort

loin du rire

des bourreaux

Ici

Schirmeck

Éternellement

Ici

éternellement

Jo.

RITA GABBAI-SIMANTOV

Rita Gabbai-Simantov lives in Athens. Her family is of Sephardic-Turkish ancestry.

SILENCE

Where are you going, man,
lost in the streets
of old Saloniki?
Neither those neighbourhoods
nor courtyards
nor story-telling on the Sabbath
exist any longer.
As you walk, your companion
will be silence.

Translated from the Ladino by Anna Crowe

SILENCIO

Hombre, ¿ánde vas
pedrido en las calles
del viejo Salonic?
Ya no existen más
ni vicintados
ni cortijos
ni cuentos de sabat.
Compañero en tu vuelta
será el silencio.

YORGOS KAFTANTZIS

All the Jews of Kaftantzis' native town of Serres in Greek Macedonia were deported to Treblinka in 1943. Kaftantzis (1920-1998) fought in the Greek National Resistance.

ROZA MIRALAI

Roza Miralai, daughter of Judas
what are you after in these
thick mists and the stark twilight.
You mustn't keep returning
with your fixed gaze
all depth and serenity
and the yellow star on your hollow breast.

The terrible smoke of your flesh
burns the memory in empty rooms
with all our old fears.
Yet this sorrow is no longer yours.

O, time passes and I sing of you
elusive like the wind, and like a shadow empty
vainly seeking your form
in the water's wide-open eyes
the silence's yellow deluges
of pristine death and ecstatic dawns.

Translated from the Greek by David Connolly

ΡΟΖΑ ΜΙΡΑΛΑΪ

Ρόζα Μιραλάι, θυγατέρα του Γιουδά
τί ζητάς εσύ ανάμεσα σ' αυτές
τις πηχτές καταχνιές και το άγριο λυκόφωτο.
Δεν πρέπει να ξαναγυρίζεις κάθε τόσο
με το ασάλευτό σου βλέμμα
όλο βάθος και γαλήνη
και το κίτρινο αστέρι στο κούφιο στήθος.

Ο τρομερός καπνός της σάρκας σου
καίει τη μνήμη σ' άδειες κάμαρες
με όλους τους παλιούς μας φόβους.
Μα η θλίψη αυτή δεν είναι πια δική σου.

Ω, άπιαστη σαν αγέρας, αδειανή σα σκιά
φεύγει ο καιρός και γω σε τραγουδώ
αναζητώντας μάταια τη μορφή σου
στα ορθάνοιχτα μάτια του νερού
και στις κίτρινες πλημμυρίδες της σιγής
από καθάριο θάνατο κι εκστατικά χαράματα.

IDA GERHARDT

Gerhardt was a Dutch poet, born in 1905. She had many Jewish friends who were murdered and she felt guilty because of this. She died in 1997. Anne Frank's statue by Pieter d'Hont was placed on Janskerkhof square in Utrecht in 1960. Flowers are laid there all year round.

THE REJECTED GIFT

It was winter and the city wrapped in dusk.
I meant to walk across *Janskerkhof*
really just to lay some flowers
I had intended for Anne Frank.
I had already taken the paper off,
but stepped back. The statue on the square
in this twilight was alive and stared at me
and her silent lips wanted to speak to me
while, unmoving, I just kept standing there.
Nothing disturbed this untemporal encounter.
Until I heard her wordless accusation,
she, a Jewish child hurt by all the centuries before:
'You were with them. Even now that she is no more.'

Translated from the Dutch by Marian de Vooght

DE TERUGGEWEZEN GAVE

't Was winter en al schemerig in de stad.
Ik wilde het Janskerkhof over gaan,
eigenlijk om bij Anne Frank te leggen
een bosje bloemen dat ik bij mij had.
Ik had ze al van het papier ontdaan,
maar week terug. Het beeldje op het plein
in deze schemering leefde en zag mij aan
en stille lippen wilden mij iets zeggen,

terwijl ik onbewegelijk bleef staan.
Niets stoorde dit ontijdelijk samenzijn.
Tot hoorbaar werd haar woordenloos vermaan,
zij, een Joods kind dat weet van eeuwen heeft:
'Gij waart daarbij. Ook nu zij niet meer leeft.'

GUNVOR HOFMO

Hofmo was from a working class family with communist sympathies. As well as her lover Ruth Maier, whose voice Hofmo kept hearing after she was murdered in Auschwitz (see the note for 'Encounter', p. 121), the poet's brother was also deported, to Sachsenhausen, but he survived.

TO ONE WHO USED TO BE

Always your quiet voice,
the bird that glides away
through faraway-light images
by which the distance hurts.
The world opens softly
a pine tree wet with evening speaks
to the sorrow and the light, and tenderness
is full of moss and earth.

That's why longing listens,
that's why peace is fleeing
in this burnt-down daily life
to which I cannot reconcile.
The world is your eyes,
the world is your mouth.
Time and again I stand in it blind.
But *you* give me a moment's sight.

Translated from the Norwegian by Marian de Vooght

TIL EN SOM VAR

Alltid din stille stemme,
fuglen som glir avsted
gjennom de lysfjerne bilder
avstanden såres ved.
Tingene åpner seg sakte,
en kveldsvåt furu får ord
til sorgen i lyset, og ømhet
brister av mose og jord.

Derfor den lyttende lengsel,
derfor den flyktende fred
i denne forbrente hverdag
jeg aldri forsones med.
Tingene er dine øyne,
tingene er din munn.
Blind står jeg ofte iblant dem.
Men *du* er min seende stund.

ED. HOORNIK

*Hoornik was arrested in 1943 for publishing illegally. He was imprisoned
in camp Vught in the Netherlands, and then deported to Dachau in May
1944. After Dachau was liberated by the Americans in April 1945,
Hoornik suffered lifelong trauma.*

THE SURVIVOR

I
A tall man in a zebra jacket.
His eyes are burning in the rain.
He hides his head, just bags it.

Arms spread out like branches,
he drags himself, a wooden bird.
I hear it snap when he collapses.

II
Drawn-out wisps of smoke
leave the chimney daily;
Greco-esque figures,
finger-like.

They twist and swirl,
stumble and dwindle,
to nothing,
to death.

III
I am the survivor,
the dead one who didn't die,
the dog howling at the moon.

I crawl under the table,
my head between my paws
my mouth a mouth full of blood.

Translated from the Dutch by Marian de Vooght

DE NABESTAANDE

I
Een lange man in zebrapak.
Zijn ogen branden in de regen.
Hij doet zijn hoofd weg in een zak.

Armen als takken uitgestrekt,
sleept hij zich voort, een houten vogel.
Ik hoor het knakken als hij valt.

II
Iedere dag komt uit de schoorsteen
in lange slierten de rook;
als Greco-figuren,
als vingers.
Ze kronkelen en draaien,
kantelen en verwaaien,
tot niets,
tot dood.

III
Ik ben de nabestaande,
de ongestorven dode,
de hond die naar de maan huilt.

Ik kruip onder de tafel,
mijn kop tussen mijn poten,
mijn bek een bek vol bloed.

BARBARA LIPINSKA-LEIDINGER

Born in Warsaw in 1953, Lipinska has lived as a film director and scriptwriter in Germany since 1977. Her father was in the Polish Resistance and was sent to Stutthof concentration camp. Her poems form part of a cycle reflecting on the making of her 1998 film about the Euthanasia programme, Transport in den Tod *(Death Transport).*

LETTERS FROM RELATIVES

"… since it's mortifying, as a mother,
not to know
where her child is…
awaiting your earliest reply
… I remain…"

There remains
a mother with her "Heil Hitler"
helpless
the ink still seems so fresh
I could smudge it with a tear
I'll keep it to myself
it is mortifying to know
where her daughter is
and the return stamp remains unused
where is the answer…

Translated from the German by Jean Boase-Beier

BRIEFE DER ANGEHÖRIGEN

„…da es einer Mutter doch peinlich ist
nicht zu wissen
wo sich ihr Kind befindet…
eine Antwort baldigst erwartend
… verbleibt…"

zurück bleibt
eine Mutter mit ihrem „Heil Hitler"
hilflos
die Tinte wirkt noch so frisch

ich könnte sie mit einer Träne verwischen
ich behalte sie für mich
es ist mir peinlich zu wissen
wo sich ihre Tochter befindet
und das Rückporto liegt immer noch bei
wo verbleibt die Antwort …

STANISLAV SMELYANSKY

See the note on the poet preceding the poem 'Dancing Gypsy', p. 102.

RAILWAY

The railway to nowhere.
And smoke. And stench. And moaning.
The railway to neverland.
And smoke. And overcrowded carriages.

And smoke. And no shadows anymore.
Passengers looking sternly.
And there by the Moon, round the corner
the railway disappearing …

Translated from the Russian by Veronika Krasnova

ДОРОГА

Железная дорога в никуда.
И дым. И вонь. И жалобные стоны.
Железная дорога в никогда.
И дым. И переполнены вагоны.

И дым. И тени больше не видны.
Соседи по вагону смотрят строго.
И там, за поворотом у луны,
Теряется железная дорога…

RIVKA BASMAN BEN-HAYIM

Basman Ben-Hayim, who was born in 1925, spent two years in the Vilna ghetto in Lithuania, from where she was sent to the forced-labour camp Kaiserwald. There she wrote poems in micrography, and saved them on a piece of paper rolled up under her tongue when the camp was liquidated. After the war, she continued to recall her experiences in poetry.

SOMETIMES A HUNGER GRIPS ME...

Sometimes a hunger grips me
As in those days
When we grasped a teeny bite.
I am frightened by this.
There is bread in my house
Far more than enough.
Then why the sudden
Ravenous hunger-call?
Probably
So I should not forget –

Translated from the Yiddish by Zelda Kahan Newman

ES TREFT IN MIR A HUNGER...

Es treft in mir a hunger
vi in yene teg
fun oysgeyn nokh a bisn;
Ikh dershrek zikh far aza gefil.
Faran iz broyt in shtub
genuk tsu esn,
to vi pasirt in mitn heln tog
aza min hungerike hunger?
Min-hastam
oyf nit fargesn.

RAJZEL ZYCHLINSKI

Zychlinski, whose mother, brothers, sister, nephews and nieces were murdered in Chelmno and Treblinka, kept coming back to this loss in her poetry for the rest of her life. Also see the note for Zychlinski's poem 'Prayer', p. 43.

IT COULD BE...

it could be
I saw doctor mengele today
drinking a glass of beer
in tel-aviv
by the sea –
a pair of blue sharp eyes
suddenly flashed over at me
with a cold steel gleam like knives.
from his mouth a false artificial laugh
suddenly woke the horror up –
left, right, left, right,
left! – – –
to the gas!– – –
politely he introduced himself
to the people at the table next to me –
his family are english, scottish,
and on his mother's side
he is german.
I moved away from the cool terrace
and walked around a long time in the heat,
by the sea –
and heard the waves mimicking
german, german, german – – –

Translated from the Yiddish by Jean Boase-Beier

SS'KEN SAJN...

ss'ken sajn
ich hob hajnt gesen dokter mengele
trinken a glos bir
in tel-aviv
bajm jam –
a por bloje scharfe ojgn
hobn pluzling a bliz geton zu mir
mit a kaltn schtolenem glanz fun messerss.
a gemacht un falsch gelechterl fun sajn mojl
hot pluzling ojfgewekt dem grojl –
linkss, rechtss, linkss, rechtss,
linkss! – – –
zum gas! – – –
heflech hot er sich forgeschtelt
far di schchejnim fun majn tischl –
er schtamt fun englender, sskotn,
un fun der muterss zad
is er dojtsch.
ich bin awek fun der kiler terasse
un sich noch lang arumgedrejt in der hiz,
bajm jam –
un gehert di chwaljess nochkrimen –
dojtsch, dojtsch, dojtsch – – –

VOLDEMARS AVENS

*Avens, born in 1924, is a Latvian emigrant to the United States; he wrote
this poem during a trip back to Riga. Blue buses were Swedish-made Riga
transit vehicles used by Nazi collaborator Viktors Arājs and his commando
to travel around the country to find Jews and other unwanted people, who
were then murdered.*

THE BLUE BUSES

Maybe someday you ought to
get on a slow, blue bus.
To climb in through the back door,
and let a stiff-collared conductor
punch a hole in your conscience.
        And then,
as the journey begins,

through a crack in the floor
silently follow the road.
That way, some grayish morning
as you quietly tour the city of Riga,
winding the film in your camera,
you will arrive at the people's veins,
and learn what not everyone knows,
what only the blue buses knew.

Translated from the Latvian by Bitite Vinklers

ZILIE AUTOBUSI

Tev varbūt kādreiz vajadzētu
kāpt lēnā, zilā autobusā.
Pa pakaļdurvīm iekāpt vāģī,
ļaut konduktoram cietā krāgā
kniebt caurumu tev sirdsapziņā.
    Un tad,
uz priekšu ceļu šķirot,
no klusas šķirbas grīdu vērot
(un pagātnes tev nav un nebūs).
Tā, palsā rītā filmu griežot
un apceļojot Rīgu klusi,
tu nokļūsi pie tautas vēnām
un ziņām tām, ko nezin visi,
ko zin tik zilie autobusi.

RIVKA BASMAN BEN-HAYIM

See the note for 'Sometimes a Hunger Grips Me', p. 142. Imprisoned in Kaiserwald, Basman Ben-Hayim performed her poems for inmates together with a singer, Tsirl, and the world-renowned dancer, Musye Daykhes.

SIXTY YEARS LATER

We didn't play with time –
We played endlessly
With death.
We met it with caution
Every day.
We were young,

Merely children,
We held onto life
Unbidden.
We held within us the breath of home
In the step of spring.
And our gloom
Preserved our yesterdays.
We never spoke of the future.
We were hungry
Dreamed of bread and thick soup
And when one of us requested
"A good word",
A hungry look silently answered
"Bread."
Those days, when the scent of bread
Wafted by only in a dream.
God, too, wore a yellow star, –
How then could He save His children?
We didn't play with time behind barbed wired
There life was forbidden.
At night, when one of us stood watch in the doorway,
Musye danced spring for us.
We read and swallowed one poem after another,
And the words kissed and stroked us,
And a tear of comfort
Spoke to us within the poem.
Then a hungry voice called out:
"Oy, read it again."
And those of us who reached a shore
Wounded,
Seemed to be whole,
But there was no one out there
To hear the story, one that had
No end,
Eternally not healed.
And now we are the last witnesses on earth
Who saw and heard it all,
And when we meet in houses,
How good to feel a hand that survived,
How good the gaze that smiles through a tear –

A tear entirely different,
A sweet tear for all that lives –
For our being children and family
In the day that promises and hopes
And grows and thrives,
And carries all along with it.

Translated from the Yiddish by Zelda Kahan Newman

ZEKHTSIK YOR SHPETER

Mir hobn nit geshpilt zikh mit der tsayt.
Mir hobn zikh geshpilt keseder
Mitn toyt.
Forzikhtik bagegnt im
Fun tog tsu tog.
Mir zaynen yung geven,
Nokh kinder.
Geklamert zikh in lebn
On keynems a bafel.
Getrogn in zikh otems fun a heym
In frilingdike trit,
Un s'hot der umet
Undz gehit dem nekhtn.
Mir hobn keyn mol nit geret mit zikh
Fun tsukunft.
Mir zaynen hungerik geven,
Gekholomt fun gedikhter zup mit broyt.
Az eyner hot fun indz gebetn
"A gutn vort", –
Hot shtilerheyt a hungeriker blik ge'enfert:
"A labn broyt".
In yener tsayt, ven bloyz in kholem
Hot geshmekt fun broyt,
Hot got aleyn gehat oyf zikh a geyle late.
To vi azoy hot er gekent di kinder zayne
Rateven fun toyt?!
Mir hobn nit geshpilt zikh mit der tsayt ahinter
    shtekhldrotn
Vu lebn iz geven farbotn.
Bay nakht, az eyne hot baym tir gehit,
Hot Musye far undz oysgetantst far undz dem friling, –
Mir flegn leyenen un shlingen lid nokh lid
Un verter hobn undz gekusht, geglet
Un s'hot a groyse trer fun treyst
In lid tsu undz geret.

Demolt flegt a hungeriker kol a flister ton:
"Oy, leyenen nokh amol".
Ver fun undz hot glik gehat farvundikt kumen
Tsu a breg,
Ke'ilu vi farheylt,
Iz nit geven in droysn
Ver es zol derhern di dertseylung , a mayse on a
Sof,
Oyf eybik on a heylung.
Un itster zaynen mir di letste eydes oyf der erd
Vos hobn alts aleyn gezen, gehert,
Un az mir trefn zikh in heymen dort baynand,
Vi gut iz filn a geratevete hant,
A blik vos shmeykhlt mit a trer,
A trer mit gor an ander meyn,
A zise trer far alts vos lebt,
Far undzer zayn mit kint un keyt,
In tog vos leybedikerheyt zogt tsu un hoft
Un vakst un blit, –
Un nemt zey ale mit.

EDITH BRUCK

After the liberation in 1945, Bruck experienced continued discrimination as a survivor, first in her native Hungary and then in Czechoslovakia, before she was finally able to settle in Italy. Also see the note for Bruck's poem 'Arrival', p. 70.

THE SIGN

She died of helplessness
you can write it on my tomb
who knows where, there's no guarantee
that one dies in the place one was born or lived
one can be anywhere
in this uncertain time
there's no bad ground and good ground
but I would like as a marker a small star
with six points like that which shone
in childhood on my threadbare coat
carved well into the stone
like the one they carved in me on my skin
in my flesh and in my guts

and if there is another life
I will be a yellow star
to remind you that once there was
Auschwitz.

Translated from the Italian by Peter Ualrig Kennedy

IL SEGNO

Morì d'impotenza
si potrà scrivere sulla mia tomba
chissà dove, non è detto che uno muore
nel luogo in cui è nato o vive
si può essere dovunque
in quell'ora incerta
non ci sono terre cattive e terre buone
vorrei però come segno una piccola stella
a sei punte come quella che da bambina
brillava sul cappottino liso
incidetela ben bene nella pietra
come l'hanno incisa in me sulla mia pelle
nella mia carne nelle mie viscere
e se ci sarà un' altra vita
sarò una stella gialla
per ricordarvi che c'era una volta
Auschwitz.

JEAN CAYROL

Born in 1911 in Bordeaux, Cayrol was a member of the French Resistance, and was sent to Mauthausen concentration camp. 'O mes morts' is a section of his long poem 'Cantiques du feu' (Canticles of the Fire), written in June 1945 as a memorial to his brother Pierre and all the others killed in the camps. Cayrol died in 2005.

O MY DEAD...

O my dead you return upon our heads like tongues of fire
and it's you who will loosen our tongues
in the smallest lost valleys of our memories.

Your presence is a stream in us like the first rain of mercy
in a sky paralyzed by the brutality of your death
there is no patch of soil which would not be bound to endure

your lost future, your burnt tomorrows
there is no corn that would not be tied by your two hands
there is no love that would not fall dumb in your scorched silence
"Go! Tell the world that we are the ancient smile of the prisons
the wandering wound, the perplexing scar illuminated
that opens its wings like a bird
forgiveness
the time is near in which one will not be able to think of you
    without crying
in which we will come to found our own death in the brotherhood
heart-rending scent of the rejuvenating meadows
each one of you will be the rock for the supreme edifice
of our agony
of the agony of a world grown old in the beaten
blood of vagabond nights
that find you back at the first bell that sounds the harvest..."

Translated from the French by Marian de Vooght & Jean Boase-Beier

O MES MORTS...

O mes morts vous revenez sur nos têtes comme des langues
    de Feu
et c'est vous qui allez nous délier la langue
dans les moindres vallées perdues de nos mémoires

Votre présence ruisselle en nous comme la première pluie
    de la Miséricorde
dans le ciel paralysé par la rudesse de votre mort
il n'est pas un coin de terre qui ne doive supporter
votre avenir errant vos lendemains calcinés
il n'est pas un blé qui ne soit lié par vos deux mains
il n'est pas un amour qui ne se taise dans votre silence brûlé
«Allez dites au monde que nous sommes l'ancien sourire des
    prisons
la Blessure errante illuminée la Plaie rêveuse
qui se déploie comme un oiseau
le pardon
le temps approche où l'on ne pourra vous regarder sans
    pleurer
où nous viendrons fonder notre propre mort dans la
    fraternité

odeur pathétique des prairies renaissantes
chacun de vous sera la pierre pour l'édifice suprême
de notre agonie de l'agonie d'un monde vieilli dans le sang
    fouetté de nuits vagabondes
qui vous retrouvent à la première cloche qui sonne la
    moisson…»

GEORG EDLER VON BORIS

*Though this poem was written in the Flossenbürg concentration camp,
a forced-labour camp in the South-East of Germany, the poet imagines
remembering the horror afterwards.*

SONGS OF HORROR

The dying were telling…
Of the hours
Of beating and flaying
Of torment and torture.
And everything that I saw
I ban to my songs of horror.
What the old men said,
Who, in the days that remained,
Kept the Reaper out of mind.
What, in the bright morning,
Naked children were whispering,
Not caring if Father Death came knocking.
What the heroes tell us.
What the graves let us guess.
Every reminder of what I saw…
I move to my songs of horror.

Translated from the German by Philip Wilson

DIE LIEDER DES GRAUENS

Was in den Stunden,
In denen sie gefoltert und gequält,
Geschlagen und geschunden,
Mir die Sterbenden erzählt,
Bann ich im Erleben des Beschauens,

In die Lieder meines Grauens.
Was mir Greise sagen,
Die in ihren alten Tagen,
Nach dem Sensenmann nicht fragen.
Was in hellen Morgenschimmern,
Nackte Kinder wimmern,
Die sich um Gevatter Hein nicht kümmern.
Was die Helden melden
Und die Gräber lassen ahnen,
All das Mahnen des Beschauens,
Faß ich in die Lieder meines Grauens.

CEIJA STOJKA

Stojka was an Austrian painter and writer, born in 1933. A member of the Lovari, who are Roma horse traders, she was deported to Auschwitz-Birkenau in 1943. She survived several camps, but most of her extended family were murdered. She died in 2013.

AUSCHWITZ IS MY OVERCOAT

you are afraid of the darkness?
i can tell you, when there's no one on the road,
you have nothing to fear.

i am not afraid.
my fear stayed behind in auschwitz
and in the camps.

auschwitz is my overcoat,
bergen-belsen my dress
and ravensbrück my vest.
what is there to fear?

Translated from the German by Marian de Vooght & Jean Boase-Beier

AUSCHWITZ IST MEIN MANTEL

du hast angst vor der finsternis?
ich sage dir, wo der weg menschenleer ist,
brauchst du nichts zu fürchten.

ich habe keine angst.
meine angst ist in auschwitz geblieben
und in den lagern.

auschwitz ist mein mantel,
bergen-belsen mein kleid
und ravensbrück mein unterhemd.
wovor soll ich mich fürchten?

JÓZSEF CHOLI DARÓCZI

Daróczi was a well-known Roma poet, writer and educator, who was born in 1939 in Bedő, Hungary, and died in 2018. A kopja post is a traditional Transylvanian-Hungarian carved wooden post marking graves, recently expropriated by the nationalist Right in Hungary, as an alternative to traditional Christian symbols.

IN MEMORY OF THE GYPSY VICTIMS OF THE HOLOCAUST

The road came to a dead end in Auschwitz-Birkenau.
The earth erupted, God's sky was darkened with fire.
For God too was orphaned at the Gypsy Lager Gate,
like black fire
like black fire.
The freshly dug grave-ditches were left empty.
Our dead were shot and dumped
in the Drava and Duna
in the Vistula and the Tisza.
Our dead lie without epitaph.
Who now tends or remembers their unmarked graves?
They don't speak, silent and empty
are the coffins and graveyards.
They let our dead float away
like piles of felled logs.
There are no marked or unmarked gypsy graves
And no one remembers any more
Why?
Only the scorched earth.
Only the scorched earth.
Though there were Gypsy soldiers too

Who froze at the Don Bend.
Did God prepare a welcome in His country
for those Gypsy souls that rose
from the smoke of the crematoria?
Do they sit at the Father's right hand?
Beneath the outstretched arms of the crucified Christ?
Or do the *kopja* posts
there too trample over the simple wooden cross?
The victim Gypsy souls,
there too, as on earth, Lord,
do they fail to find a manger and a roof?

Then where is Your power, pray,
where is Your power?

Translated from the Hungarian by Jamie McKendrick, George Gömöri & Mari Gömöri

A HOLOKAUSZT CIGÁNY ÁLDOZATAINAK EMLÉKÉRE

Auschwitz-Birkenauban megrekedt az út,
Felforrt a föld, és lángba borult az Isten ege,
Mert az Isten is elárvut a cigány tábor kapujában,
Mint a fekete tűz,
Mint a fekete tűz.
Üresen maradtak a megásott sírgödrök,
Mert halottainkat a
Drávába, a
Dunába, a
Visztulába, és a Tiszába lőtték!
Jelöletlenül nyugszanak halottaink!
Kik emlékcznck a jeltelen sírokra?
Hallgatnak, némák az üresen maradt koporsók,
Az üres temetök.
Halottainkat elúsztatták,
Mint a szálfát.
Nincsenek sem jelzett, sem jeltelen cigány sírok,
És ninczenek már emlékek sem!
Miért?
Csak a felperzselt föld,
Csak a felperzselt föld.
Pedig cigány baka is megfagyott a Don-kanyarban!
Isten befogadta országába
A krematórium füstjével hozzá felszálló cigány lelkeket?
Ott ülnek az Atya jobbján,
Jézus kifeszített karjai alatt?
Vagy az oszlopos kopjafák

Ott is eltapossák a
Deszkakereszteket?
A feláldozott cigány lelkek
Ott sem lelik meg a jászolnyi hazát
Uram?

Hát milyen a Te erőd,
Milyen a Te erőd?

NELLY SACHS

See the note for Sachs's poem 'They no longer weep and wail…', p. 80.

YOU BYSTANDERS…

You bystanders
Under whose gaze murder was done.
Just as we feel an eye-gaze from behind,
So you feel in your bodies
The gaze of the dead.

How many breaking eyes will stare at you
When you pick a violet from its hiding-place?
How many pleading lifted hands
In the martyred knotted branches
Of the old oaks?
How much memory grows in the blood
Of the evening sun?

Oh, the unsung lullabies
In the night-call of a turtledove –
Some of them could have pulled down stars,
But now the old well must do it for them.

You bystanders,
You who never raised a hand to kill,
But who let the dust remain on your longing,
Not shaken off,
Who stand still, there – where it changes
To light.

Translated from the German by Jean Boase-Beier

IHR ZUSCHAUENDEN…

Ihr Zuschauenden
Unter deren Blicken getötet wurde.
Wie man auch einen Blick im Rücken fühlt,
So fühlt ihr an euerm Leibe
Die Blicke der Toten.

Wieviel brechende Augen werden euch ansehn
Wenn ihr aus den Verstecken ein Veilchen pflückt?
Wieviel flehend erhobene Hände
In dem märtyrerhaft geschlungenen Gezweige
Der alten Eichen?
Wieviel Erinnerung wächst im Blute
Der Abendsonne?

O die ungesungenen Wiegenlieder
In der Turteltaube Nachtruf –
Manch einer hätte Sterne herunterholen können,
Nun muß es der alte Brunnen für ihn tun!

Ihr Zuschauenden,
Die ihr keine Mörderhand erhobt,
Aber die ihr den Staub nicht von eurer Sehnsucht
Schütteltet,
Die ihr stehenbliebt, dort, wo er zu Licht
Verwandelt wird.

JANINA DEGUTYTĖ

The Lithuanian poet and teacher Degutytė, born in Kaunas in 1928, put the place she visited underneath the poem: Osvencimas (Auschwitz). She died in Vilnius in 1990.

AUSCHWITZ HAIR

… I too walked here. On stones – like coals.
… My limbs still shaking from fever and chills.
… I too did not return, reduced to dust and smoke.
In a cell with hair I search for my hair.

Oh we come from far.
… From Mammoth hunts,
From dancing, crying Pompeii

set in stone.
From shipwrecked Viking ships,
the battlefield of Žalgiris,
from huts of serfs,
                              conscription camps,
                              Siberia...
From Castilian squares,
                    from forts
                              from ghettoes...
Oh, we have come from far –
in search of our hair and bones...

The stones are gleaming in the autumn sun...
        Lips gasp for air...
The only sound is the rustling of golden leaves,
        The rustling flow of time:
        which was – is – will be...

Translated from the Lithuanian by M. G. Slavėnas

OSVENCIMO PLAUKAI

        ... Ir aš čia ėjau... Tie akmenys – kaip žarijos.
        ... Ir krečia dar visą kūną nuo šalčio ir skausmo...
        ... Ir aš iš čia negrįžau, pavirtus dulkėm ir dūmais.
    Ir kameroj, pilnoj plaukų, aš ieškau savo...
            O mes iš taip toli atėjom.
                ... Iš mamutų medžioklės,
            Iš suakmenėjusios verkiančios ir
            šokančios Pompėjos,
            Iš sudužusio vikingų laivo
            ir Žalgirio,
            Iš baudžiauninkų lūšnų,
                                rekrūtų
                                ir sibirų...
            Iš Kastilijos aikščių,
                        iš fortų
                                ir getų...
            O mes iš taip toli atėjom –
            ieškoti savo plaukų ir kaulų...
        ... O rudenio saulė blyksi ant akmenų...
            O lūpoms dar maža ir maža vėjo...
    Ir šlama geltoni medžiai,
            Ir šlama laikas:
            Buvęs – esamas – būsimas...

TAMARA KAMENSZAIN

Kamenszain was born in 1949 in Buenos Aires. The exploration of her Jewish roots and the word, language and art as a place of shelter are recurring themes in her poetry.

I HAVEN'T EVER TOLD ANY OF MY THERAPISTS THIS...

I haven't ever told any of my therapists this:
at my Jewish primary school every year we'd watch
the same film about the Nazi concentration camps
the one where some living corpses dig a pit
then toss into it the little bones of their dead
and then are even forced
to shove each other in – a suicide by others
who shoot them dead so light they just drop
without really knowing how.
Don't know why but still today when a taxi driver says
anything about the Jews I keep shtum
in case he might see me through the rear view mirror
also standing on the edge of that pit.
So I say nothing but instead hide
behind the first person.

Translated from the Spanish by Cecilia Rossi

ESTO NO SE LO CONTÉ NUNCA A NINGUNO DE MIS ANALISTAS...

Esto no se lo conté nunca a ninguno de mis analistas:
en el colegio primario judío veíamos todos los años
la misma película de los campos de concentración nazi
esa donde unos cadáveres vivos cavan la fosa
después tiran adentro los huesitos de sus muertos
y después todavía son obligados
a empujarse a sí mismos suicidados por otros
que los fusilan para que de tan livianitos caigan
sin comerla ni beberla.
No sé pero todavía hoy cuando un taxista dice
algo sobre los judíos me callo
no vaya a ser que por el espejo retrovisor descubra
que yo también estoy al borde de esa fosa.
Por eso no opino por eso me escondo
detrás de la primera persona.

See the note above for 'I haven't ever told any of my therapists this'. Transit camp Terezín was used by the Nazis as a so-called model Jewish settlement for propaganda purposes. Artists, actors, musicians and intellectuals were imprisoned there before further deportation, mostly to Auschwitz.

THE ARTISTS DETAINED AT TEREZÍN...

The artists detained at Terezín
produced two kinds of drawings:
those demanded by the Reich to promote the camps
and the forbidden ones they hid inside their tattered bags.
Two sides of reality. Which is the more realistic?
Because they seemed very clear that the end of their lives
would also be a prophecy of the end of the world.
For this and only this they worked in duplicate:
below the forced fiction of their labour
in the most intimate carbon copy of their private papers,
they found through free association a *via regia*
a Freudian way out.
In this way they denied the dreadful phrase
because no work sets you free except for that which nothing
and nobody forces you to do.

Translated from the Spanish by Cecilia Rossi

LOS ARTISTAS PRESOS EN TEREZÍN...

Los artistas presos en Terezín
hicieron dos tipos de dibujos:
los que el Reich les exigía para promocionar los campos
y los prohibidos que ellos escondían
entre sus ajados bártulos.
Dos caras de la realidad. ¿Cuál es la más realista?
Porque ellos parecían tener muy claro que el fin de sus vidas
iba a ser también una profecía del fin del mundo.
Por eso y sólo por eso trabajaron con copia:
debajo de la ficción forzada que les impusieron,
en el íntimo carbónico de sus papeles privados,
encontraron por asociación libre una vía regia
un agujero freudiano de salida.
Así desmintieron la frase nefasta
porque ningún trabajo libera salvo que nada ni nadie
nos obligue a hacerlo.

BARBARA LIPINSKA-LEIDINGER

Hadamar is a hospital in the West of Germany, where around 14,000 people were killed, because they were mentally ill, or thought to be ill, or because they were exempt from deportation (for example, the Jewish children of mixed marriages). Also see the comment for Lipinska-Leidinger's poem 'Letters from Relatives', p. 140.

HADAMAR

It is cold
impossible to show
I turn on the spot
on the chessboard of death
in the gas chamber
I breathe deeply
hold up...

Translated from the German by Jean Boase-Beier

HADAMAR

Es ist kalt
unmöglich zu zeigen
ich drehe mich auf der Stelle
auf dem Schachbrett des Todes
in der Gaskammer
atme ich tief durch
aushalten...

WERNER DÜRRSON

Dürrson was born in 1932 and died in 2008. Here he writes about the fate of the 10,654 people with disabilities, brought to Grafeneck Castle in Baden-Württemberg in 1940 from care institutions in the South-West of Germany and murdered in a newly-built gas chamber. This was the first location of the Euthanasia programme.

GRAFENECK

Reaching upwards limes horse-chestnuts
airy avenue
the sky pristine blue
unhindered view to hilly distances

> I see you see
> the Spring is mild

No fluttering tape in the wind no
breath nothing rises from the meadows
I ask you ask who
carted the souls up there
ten thousand times delivered bread
to worthless eaters they
don't starve for long

> I feel you feel
> the Spring is soft

Upwards through limes horse-chestnuts the
smoke plume high who turned
the tap on stoked the fire
threw them in who washed
their hands with soap it
did not scream did not foam

> sleep lovely sleep
> ten thousand times you see
> the Spring is blind

I ask you ask no-one knows
black fluttering in the wind the
sky greyer than grey who
shoved the slack to one side
swept the ashes into a pile who
dug the ditch sowed the grass

> I hear you hear the witnesses
> do not talk
> the Spring is sly

Closely drawn in the rows
limes horse-chestnuts lovely avenue
the sky pristine clear
no fluttering tape in the wind no
hair solid green nothing
rises from the meadows

> the birds twitter
> the Spring is blue

Translated from the German by Jean Boase-Beier

GRAFENECK

Bergaufwärts Linden Kastanien
lichte Allee
der Himmel feinsäuberlich blau
klare Sicht in hüglige Fernen

> ich sehe du siehst
> der Frühling ist mild

Kein flatterndes Band im Wind kein
Hauch nichts steigt aus den Wiesen
ich frage du fragst wer
karrte die Seelen hinauf
zehntausendfach lieferte Brot
unnützen Essern die
hungern nicht lang

ich spüre du spürst
der Frühling ist lau

Aufwärts durch Linden Kastanien die
Rauchfahne hoch wer drehte
den Hahn auf schürte das Feuer
warf sie hinein wer wusch sich
die Hände mit Seife die
schrie nicht schäumte nicht

Schlaf schöner Schlaf
zehntausendfach siehst du
der Frühling ist blind

ich frage du fragst niemand weiß
schwarzes Flattern im Wind der
Himmel grauer als grau wer
schob die Schlacke beiseite
kehrte die Asche zusammen wer
grub die Grube säte das Gras

ich höre du hörst die Zeugen
schweigen
der Frühling ist schlau

Dicht geschlossen die Reihen
Linden Kastanien schöne Allee
der Himmel feinsäuberlich klar
kein flatterndes Band im Wind kein
Haar sattes Grün nichts
steigt aus den Wiesen

die Vögel zwitschern
der Frühling ist blau

BARBARA LIPINSKA-LEIDINGER

This poem refers to the second phase of the Nazi Euthanasia killings, when, after the programme's official end in 1941, murder continued by medical overdoses, neglect and starvation in centres like the Obrawalde hospital in what was then German Meseritz, now Międzyrzecz in Western Poland. See the note for 'Letters from Relatives', p. 140.

MESERITZ / MIĘDZYRZECZ

What did you really know
you neighbours of the condemned
Over-the-fence talk
was prohibited
you were ashamed
as the Russians shot Ratajczak
"She went to church every Sunday...
She was meant to care for people
not kill them..."

You're not so keen to talk of it
you neighbours of nature-lover Grabowski
who demanded brown paper from the relatives
for the clothes of the dead
and had the gravestones over the mass graves
used and reused

Behind the fence they knew everything
and the Polish patients
avoided for decades
particular house-numbers
were afraid
of the numbers of death
And still today the children
can tell stories of corpses
with glaring eyes

But no-one is so keen to talk
and also
who cares today
other worries
The raised hand of the nurse with the death-jab

has slowly faded
is sinking
beneath the glass of the memorial
It has a crack

Translated from the German by Jean Boase-Beier

MESERITZ / MIĘDZYRZECZ

Was habt ihr wirklich gewusst
Ihr Nachbarn der Todgeweihten
Es war verboten
Zaungespräche zu führen
Ihr habt euch geschämt
als die Russen die Ratajczak erschossen
„Die ging doch jeden Sonntag zur Kirche...
die sollte die Leute doch pflegen
und nicht umbringen ...“

Ihr sprecht nicht so gerne darüber
Ihr Nachbarn des Naturliebhabers Grabowski
der für die Kleidung der Toten
von den Familien Packpapier verlangte
und die Grabsteine über die Massengräbern
mehrfach verwenden ließ

Hinter dem Zaun wusste man alles
und die polnischen Patienten
mieden über Jahrzehnte
bestimmte Hausnummern
hatten Angst
vor den Todeszahlen
Und die Kinder können noch heute
Geschichten von Leichen erzählen
mit leuchtenden Augen

Aber man spricht nicht gerne darüber
und außerdem
wen kümmert es heute noch
andere Sorgen
Die erhobene Hand der Pflegerin mit der Todesspritze
ist langsam verblasst
versinkt
unterm Glas der Gedenkstätte
Es hat einen Sprung

IOSSIF VENTOURAS

Excerpts from Ventouras' long poem 'Tanaïs'. In June 1944, the Nazis forced the majority of the Cretan Jews to board the ship Tanaïs. It was bound for Piraeus from where began the train route to Auschwitz. Torpedoed by the British Navy, the Tanaïs sank in the open sea on 9 June 1944. Ventouras and his family were among the very few Jews on Crete to survive. The River Don was known to the ancient Greeks as the Tanaïs.

ORPHANED TREE OF MY SYNAGOGUE...

[...]
orphaned tree of my synagogue
which one of the dead
with cracked hand
sowed the cries of shells and shadows
in the dark depths of what seaweed
did the sun lag
and our empty houses stood derelict
deep furrows
the flesh upon flesh that drowned
nets that vanished you away
nets and a noose

*

nighttime the wind
scattered words
children's cries
moving broken branches
to the clocks' ticking
they left in the darkness
and it was
the pilot ferryman
with the river's name
pulsating container
with sirens signalling the voyage
with smells of ozone grease and rust
and still more
with the haze it was
of those others

[…]
in these waters
lives Alexander the Great
if you look at night
love is no scythe that reaps
if you look at night
you see my nights
sowing grey scales and rust
eroding the sarcophagi of the deep
if you look at night you see them all
in a choking mass
objects cast into the darkness
recollections of tales
– Pithom and Ramses –
fire and ash of our times

if you look at night you see the jinn
sealing children's bones in a chamber of steel
erasing the deep all around with sponges.
lowering the earth's levers to the screeching of gulls

    *

yet how
the letters stab
at the trough
how they record
scattered on the seabed
skull shells
it's that the light
in the crooked waves
at great risk
softens the light
rotating
and in a shade of rust
the bones' growths
sway in the glare
in opened plating
and the skulls
eyeglass skulls
cracks in the stories

[…]
The sun gilds the walls
clad in white
I'll halt at the bend
for a breath
at the ages that distant
shine in the tears
I won't look back for
life is but salt
grains of salt
in a cup I'll look at the future
faint footsteps of figures to come
light and winged they'll descend
clad in foreign clothes
on strange machines that move
when
the howling of the wind is heard
in that very same sea
just as then
when a frightful turn
deadened it by a miracle
life is but salt
grains of salt

Translated from the Greek by David Connolly

ΟΡΦΑΝΟ ΤΗΣ ΣΥΝΑΓΩΓΗΣ ΜΟΥ ΔΕΝΤΡΟ...

[…]
ορφανό της συναγωγής μου δέντρο
ποιος πεθαμένος έσπειρε
με χέρι ραγισμένο
κραυγές οστράκων και σκιές
σε ποιων φυκιών τις σκοτεινιές
ο ήλιος βραδυπόρησε,
κι' ερήμωσαν τα σπίτια μας κενά
βαθιές ήταν αυλακιές
οι σάρκες που πνιγήκαν
δίχτυα ήταν που σ' αφάνισαν
δίχτυα και θηλιά.

*

νύχτα ο άνεμος
σκορπούσε λέξεις

κλάματα παιδιών
μετακινώντας σπασμένα κλαδιά
στο κτύπο των ρολογιών
έφευγαν στο σκοτάδι
και ήταν
προπομπός πορθμέας,
του ποταμού το όνομα,
το περιέχον αυτό που πάλλει,
με τις σειρήνες που σημαίνουν το ταξίδι
με τις οσμές ιωδίου γράσου και σκουριάς
και περισσότερο
με το θαμπό εκείνων
ήταν

[...]
σε τούτα τα νερά
ζει ο Μεγαλέξανδρος
αν δεις τη νύχτα
δεν είναι ο έρωτας δρεπάνι και θερίζει
αν δεις τη νύχτα
βλέπεις τις νύχτες μου
σπέρνουν γκρίζα τα λέπια και σκουριά
διαβρώνουν τις σαρκοφάγους των βυθών
αν δεις τη νύχτα εκείνους βλέπεις
σε πνιγηρή συσσώρευση
αντικείμενα πεταμένα στο σκοτάδι
ενθυμήματα διηγήσεων
– Πιθάμ και Ρααμσές –
φωτιά και στάχτες των καιρών μας

αν δεις τη νύχτα τα τζίνι βλέπεις
σφραγίζουν οστά παιδιών σε θάλαμο χάλυβα
σβήνουν το βυθό με σπόγγους ολόγυρα.
κλείνουν οι μοχλοί της γης στο ουρλιαχτό των γλάρων

          *

μα πώς
μαχαιρώνουν τα γράμματα
στο διαθόλιο
πώς σκόρπια
καταγράφουν στο βυθό
κρανία κελύφη
είναι που το φως
στα τεθλασμένα κύματα
με κίνδυνο
μαλάσσει το φως
περιδινούμενο
και σ' απόχρωση σκουριάς

οι επιφύσεις των οστών
αιωρούνται στο θάμβος
σε ανοιγμένα ελάσματα
και τα κρανία
κρανία διόπτρες
ρωγμές στις αφηγήσεις

[...]
Ο ήλιος χρυσίζει τα τείχη
ντυμένος άσπρα
θα σταθώ στη στροφή
για μιαν ανάσα
τις εποχές που μακριά
στο δάκρυ λάμπουν
δεν θα κοιτώ γιατί
αλάτι είναι η ζωή
σταλαγματιές αλάτι
σε ένα φλιτζάνι θα κοιτώ το μέλλον
αχνές τις πατημασιές από μορφές που θα 'ρθουν
ανάλαφρες και φτερωτές θα κατεβαίνουν
ντυμένες με ρούχα ξένα
σε μηχανές αλλόκοτες που ταξιδεύουν
όταν
θ' ακούγεται το βουητό τα' ανέμου
στην ίδια εκείνη θάλασσα
όπως τότε
που φρικαλέο γύρισμα
τη νέκρωσε με θαύμα
αλάτι είναι η ζωή
σταλαγματιές αλάτι

BARBARA LIPINSKA-LEIDINGER

Victims of the Euthanasia programme were taken in grey buses to the places where they would be murdered. See the notes for Lipinska-Leidinger's poems 'Letters to Relatives' (p. 140), 'Hadamar' (p. 160) and 'Meseritz / Międzyrzecz' (p. 164).

THE JOURNEY

What landscapes did you see
on the way
the windows were painted over
so no-one could see your faces
what pictures can I show of you
your faces
I try
to hold them still
stop the old propaganda film
turn off the sound
you start to speak
you ask
Where are we going
I know
I want to go with you
I get out before you arrive
That's all I can do

Translated from the German by Jean Boase-Beier

DIE FAHRT

Welche Landschaften habt ihr gesehen
unterwegs
die Fenster waren zugestrichen
damit man Eure Gesichter nicht sieht
welche Bilder von Euch kann ich zeigen
Eure Gesichter
ich versuche
sie festzuhalten
stoppe den alten Propagandafilm
drehe den Ton ab
Ihr fangt zu sprechen an
Ihr fragt
Wohin fahren wir

ich weiß es
ich will mit
ich steige vorher aus
ich kann nicht anders

FRANCO MARCOALDI

Marcoaldi, who was born in 1955, writes here of the Eichmann trial in Jerusalem in 1961. The trial of Eichmann, who organised the logistics of the deportation of Jews and Roma to the extermination camps in minute detail, was the first Nazi trial to be televised worldwide.

THE TRAP OF EVIL: A GLIMPSE OF THE EICHMANN TRIAL

Indifferent to ridicule,
Eichmann attempts to calm
a residual tremor of conscience:
'It is my honour to be loyal',
'I am not to blame, I was an instrument,
a tool in the hands of superior forces.'
Like a drugged tiger, he repeats it,
continually stretching his mouth.
He is slave to a tic. Then slowly
he adjusts his tie,
passes his hand through his thinning hair,
dusts off the table,
polishes his glasses again and again.

In the narrow confines of the trial cage
Eichmann persists with
the same compulsion as when
onto the pages of squared paper
he numbered, one by one, the Jews
sent on their way to the slaughterhouse:

The Order was all that mattered,
and still matters, in the mulish
dullness of his brain.

Translated from the Italian by Peter Ualrig Kennedy

LA TRAPPOLA DEL MALE: UN VIDEO DEL PROCESSO EICHMANN

A sprezzo del ridicolo,
Eichmann prova a placare
un residuo sussulto di coscienza:
'il mio onore si chiama fedeltà',
'io non ho colpa, ero uno strumento
nelle mani di forze superiori'.
Lo ripete come una tigre istupidita,
stirando di continuo il labbro,
schiavo di un tic. Poi lentamente
si aggiusta la cravatta,
passa la mano tra i capelli
radi, toglie la polvere dal tavolo,
pulisce e ripulisce le lenti degli occhiali.

Nell'angusto spazio della gabbia
del processo, Eichmann rincorre
lo stesso desiderio di quando
su dei fogli quadrettati
numerava uno per uno gli ebrei
spediti in direzione del macello:

l'Ordine, solo quello contava
e conta ancora, nell'immota
ottusità del suo cervello.

ZOLTÁN SUMONYI

*Sumonyi, born in Satu Mare, Romania, in 1942, is a Hungarian poet,
writer and radio editor. Mauthausen concentration camp in Austria was
established in 1938 and initially intended to imprison criminals, political
opponents, so-called asocials and Jehovah's Witnesses.*

MAUTHAUSEN 2009

It's not the fortress walls, the battlements,
      or watch-towers of the castle, or the gate;
it's not the wreaths, or late heads bowed, too late,
      nor is it an entire nation's monuments.
It's not Death's engineering, cóvert, crafted,
      nor lawns, green-engineered, and handsome-grafted
in carpet-squares, to look as if just grown
        actually *there*. No, it's the old photos shown.

It's not the tiered bunks crammed into the gloom
    of barrack blocks. It's not the urine-drains.
It's not the shower-roses' plural bloom
    from cellar ceilings, or twin-vents for grains
of ash beneath the oven-bed's sprung coils.
    It's not the lamp that gleamed over the tiles
in the operating-theatre. These don't tell the place.
       A bunch of faded snapshots shows its real face.

It's not the corpses carted, ditched and heaped,
    or skeleton-survivors, chosen ones,
but the photos the camp-guards took, and kept,
    of one another, portly myrmidons –
smug, rosy-cheeked, these murder-orgy fellows,
    pistol cases belted on belly-pillows,
greed, lust and envy smouldering in their eyes,
       ready to rage, again, should ever chance arise.

Translated from the Hungarian by Richard Berengarten & George Gömöri

MAUTHAUSEN, 2009

1

Nem az erőd-fal, várkapu-bejárat,
    nem az őrtornyok a szögleteken,
nem a mérnöki műve a titkolt halálnak,
    nem a nemzetek emlékművei,
ahogy ma bronzban és gránitban állnak
    az éppoly mérnöki tégla-gyepen,
nem a koszorúk, a főhajtás, a kései,
    de a kiállítás képei!

2

Nem a barakkok, nem a húgy-csatorna,
    a hodályba zsúfolt priccs-emelet,
nem a pincében az a túl sok zuhanyrózsa,
    kemencékben a sodrony-ágybetét,
nem a hamuzó kétszintes torka,
    a műtő-lámpa a csempe felett,
de múzeumában egy-két sárga-szürke kép
    kimutatja rejtett lényegét.

3

Nem a futóárkokba kotort hullák,
   a túlélők, a csontváz-örömök,
de ahogy a tábor tisztjeit bemutatják:
   párnás derékon revolvertáska,
a petyhüdt arcon önelégült rózsák,
   csak a szempár sóvárgása örök –
oly ismerős; tombol, ha alkalom kínálja,
   a segéderők orgiája.

LIZZY SARA MAY

The poet's mother was murdered in Auschwitz. May, born in Sloten near Amsterdam in 1918, lived with the trauma of having survived, together with other people to whom she had offered a hiding place in her house. May died in 1988.

BLUE

Hide
because nobody should know
put your finger to your lips
when you point the finger

hide
because despair is the excess
of second-rate theatre
too many props in a light too bright

hide
because all failure is worse
than being naked
in the polished monocle of the world

hide
because what is pain
if the hats of compassion
are only tipped to the dead

Translated from the Dutch by Marian de Vooght

BLUE

Verberg je
want niemand mag het weten
leg de vinger op de lippen
als je de vinger op de wonde legt

verberg je
want wanhoop is de charge
van het slechte toneel
te veel attributen in te fel licht

verberg je
want alle mislukking is erger
dan naakt te zijn
in de geslepen monocle van de wereld

verberg je
want wat is pijn
als de hoed van mededogen
alleen voor de doden wordt afgenomen

NELO RISI

The poet empathises with his wife, Edith Bruck, who is a Holocaust survivor. Also see the note for Risi's poem 'Celan', p. 113.

BURNING

There was a place in the house
a corner of the wall where we could be
together, and just thinking about it
made one feel warm

Chimneys chimney-pots cowl
smokestack tell me the name
you psalms of light you black
phantoms from the darkness: "fireplace"
defines the passage
where the smoke escapes

Since the slow spirals
have spoken of nothing but ashes
already the fact that one exists
is a heavy burden to the survivor.

Translated from the Italian by Peter Ualrig Kennedy

STRUGGIMENTO

C'era un luogo di casa
un angolo di muro dove stare
assieme, che sola a nominarlo
emanava tepore

Ciminiere comignoli cappa
fumaiolo suggeritemi il nome
voi salmi di luce voi neri
fatasmi dal buio: "camino"
per definizione è il condotto
d'uscita del fumo

Da quando le lente volute
hanno espresso null'altro che ceneri
già il fatto di esistere
è di peso al sopravvissuto.

SAUL VAN MESSEL

In the first years of the war, van Messel (pseudonym of Jaap Meijer, 1912-1993) had been Anne Frank's history teacher at the Jewish 'Lyceum' in Amsterdam. The poet survived Bergen-Belsen but never recovered from his trauma, which is an ever-recurring theme in his often ironic poems.

SIGN
in memory of k.

death came to him
and was received
as a welcome
not uninvited guest

the neighbours mumbled
that he had hung himself

the authentic account
speaks of gassed

but strangely / not so
long ago we thought
he seemed reborn
abruptly out of gloominess

when very unexpectedly
he turned up with flowers

for the grave – in retrospect
that is – that he had dug

Translated from the Dutch by David Colmer

SIGNAAL
in memoriam k.

hem kwam de dood
en werd ontvangen
als een welkome
en niet ongenode gast

de buren mompelden
dat hij zich had verhangen
het authentiek bericht
spreekt van vergast

maar vreemd / nog niet
zo lang tevoren
scheen hij ons plotseling
uit somberheid herboren

toen hij heel onverwacht
met bloemen op kwam draven

voor het graf – dus achteraf –
dat hij al had gegraven

ROBERT DESNOS

As an active member of the French Resistance, Desnos wrote anti-Nazi poems, many in sonnet form. Because of this he was arrested in 1944 and sent as a slave-labourer to Auschwitz, dying in Terezín in 1945. This poem was written before his arrest, and anticipates the time after his death. See the note before 'Chant of the Curse', p. 71.

THE EPITAPH

I've lived today, and since antiquity
Been dead. I lived intact, but I was prey.
Man's nobler side was jailed and put away;
Among the slaves in face-masks, I was free.

I've lived today, and nonetheless been free.
I watched the river and the earth and sky
Turn round me, and they kept their harmony;
Honey and birds, a seasonal supply.

How did you use these gifts, you there alive?
Did you misuse the days I spent in toil?
Did you make common cause and till the soil
To harvest? Did you make my city thrive?

Don't fear me, you who live: I'm dead and gone:
Not soul nor body, nothing lingers on.

Translated from the French by Timothy Adès

L'ÉPITAPHE

J'ai vécu dans ces temps et depuis mille années
Je suis mort. Je vivais, non déchu mais traqué.
Toute noblesse humaine étant emprisonnée
J'étais libre parmi les esclaves masqués.

J'ai vécu dans ces temps et pourtant j'étais libre.
Je regardais le fleuve et la terre et le ciel
Tourner autour de moi, garder leur équilibre
Et les saisons fournir leurs oiseaux et leur miel.

Vous qui vivez qu'avez-vous fait de ces fortunes?
Regrettez-vous les temps où je me débattais?
Avez-vous cultivé pour des moissons communes?
Avez-vous enrichi la ville où j'habitais?

Vivants, ne craignez rien de moi, car je suis mort.
Rien ne survit de mon esprit ni de mon corps.

MOSHÉ BACHAR

Since his retirement, Bashar (born in 1936 in Tel Aviv) devotes his time to the promotion of Sephardic culture. His mother was originally from Thessaloniki and his father came from Bursa, Turkey.

YOU'LL HAVE TO LOOK FOR ME ON EVERY CORNER...

You'll have to look for me on every corner
is what my mother said to me one day
after I had made her angry.
40 years have gone by since that day
and there's not a day I don't search for her
on every corner
and not just for her
but the whole community
from the Oriental Centre, Levinski, Wolfson,
Aliyá, Herzl, Hakishón, Mizrají, Mizrají B,
the baker, the grocer, the butcher, the coachman,
and seller of boards to stand on in the bath,
the cantor, the synagogue servant, the warden,
and the Salonikan porters on their corner
with leather straps and blue numbers on their arms.
I'm searching for all of them,
and wasting my time in emptiness.

Translated from the Ladino by Anna Crowe

ME VAS A BUSCAR POR LOS CANTONES...

Me vas a buscar por los cantones
me dijo la ima un día
después que la hice eniervar.

De aquel día pasaron 40 años
y no hay día que no la busco
por todos los cantones
no sólo a ella
ma a todo el entorno
de Merkaz Misjarí, Levinski, Wolfson,
Aliyá, Herzl, Hakishón, Mizrají, Mizrají B,
al panadero, al bacal, al jasap,
al arabagí y al vendedor de tablas para el baño,
al jazán, al samás y al gabay,
a los jamales selaniclís de la quiosé
con los cusaques y los números blue en brazos.
A todos estó buscando
y pedriendo el tiempo en vacío.

ROBERT DESNOS

See the notes for Desnos' poems 'Chant of the Curse' (p. 71) and 'The Epitaph' (p. 179). Desnos wrote this poem before his arrest and detention.

THE LEGACY

Hugo! So here's your name on every wall!
Deep in the Pantheon, turn in your grave,
And ask: who's done this? Hitler! Goebbels! They've
Done it, the guttersnipes: Pétain, Laval,

Bonnard, Brinon: accomplished traitors all,
High on the hog. They've done it, and they must
Face retribution, merciless and just;
And there are not that many names at all.

These mindless and uncultured men have made
A smokescreen for their filthy escapade:
'The fellow's dead and gone,' apparently.

The fellow's dead. Yet his bequest is clear:
His legacy is signed and proven here,
Witnessed by France; we call it Liberty.

Translated from the French by Timothy Adès

LE LEGS

Et voici, Père Hugo, ton nom sur les murailles!
Tu peux te retourner au fond du Panthéon
Pour savoir qui a fait cela. Qui l'a fait? On!
On c'est Hitler, on c'est Goebbels… C'est la racaille,

Un Laval, un Pétain, un Bonnard, un Brinon,
Ceux qui savent trahir et ceux qui font ripaille,
Ceux qui sont destinés aux justes représailles
Et cela ne fait pas un grand nombre de noms.

Ces gens de peu d'esprit et de faible culture
Ont besoin d'alibis dans leur sale aventure.
Ils ont dit: "Le bonhomme est mort. Il est dompté."

Oui, le bonhomme est mort. Mais par-devant notaire
Il a bien précisé quel legs il voulait faire:
Le notaire a nom: France, et le legs: Liberté.

JACQUES PRESSER

Presser was a historian who published Ashes in the Wind: The Destruction of Dutch Jewry *in 1965. He invented the term ego-document, as he included personal stories by victims in his scholarly work. He also processed his personal suffering in his novels and poems. He died in Amsterdam in 1970.*

CON SORDINO

So he came back and once more had
To speak the language of the living,
In strangers' gardens still intact
He grew his own late-season roses,
Broke his bread at strangers' tables
After a day's work, hard as before.

He can't have been as damaged then
As other people had supposed;
They had got the wrong idea of him,
Thought him tormented by his past,
Or was he just one of those heroes,
Who go through fire and stay unharmed?

Perhaps, perhaps; he spoke that language,
He did that work; he seemed to live;
That was true too. Though now and then,
When picking roses, they said a sound
Or word could cause his hands to shiver:
But maybe that too was just a tale.

Translated from the Dutch by Donald Gardner

CON SORDINO

Zo keerde hij terug en moest
De taal der levenden weer spreken,
In vreemde tuinen onverwoest
Zijn eigen late rozen kweken,
Zijn brood aan vreemde tafels breken
Na arbeid weer als vroeger noest.

Hij was dan toch niet zo bezeerd
Als sommigen veronderstelden;
Men oordeelde ook wel verkeerd,
Dat de herinnering hem kwelde,
Of was hij toch een van die helden,
Die door een vuur gaan ongedeerd?

Misschien, misschien; hij sprak die taal,
Hij deed dat werk; hij leek te leven;
Dat was ook zo. Al deed eenmaal,
Zègt men, bij 't rozenplukken even
Een woord, een klank zijn handen beven:
Ook dat misschien maar een verhaal.

MAURITS MOK

Mok was a Dutch poet and critic, born in Haarlem in 1907, whose parents and sister were murdered in Dachau in 1944. His feelings of desolation, anger and survivor's guilt can be traced in all his work after the war, up to his last poetry collection of 1987, two years before he died.

THE FACE OF GOD AFTER AUSCHWITZ

All those souls clinging to gods,
turning spit into prayers,
warming dreams into myths,
chilling myths into rock-hard
foundations of a belief –
I push the veil from their visions
and am alone; an icy-cold gust
lifts, a horizon-wide
beat of a wing that
stirs forms and spends them,
and leaves only emptiness, wastes of snow
across the earth, a sun covered
in black and burned-out sores.

Translated from the Dutch by Marian de Vooght

THE FACE OF GOD AFTER AUSCHWITZ

Al die zielen die goden aanhangen,
speeksel omzetten in gebeden,
dromen verwarmen tot mythen,
mythen verkillen tot stenen
grondslagen van een geloof –
ik schuif de mist van hun visioenen weg
en ben alleen; een ijskoud waaien
staat op, een vleugelslag
van horizon tot horizon
die vormen oproept en verslindt,
en enkel leegte achterlaat, sneeuwvelden
over de aarde, een met zwarte, uitgegloeide
zweren overdekte zon.

LAURA RAINIERI

Italian poet Rainieri was born in 1943 and lives in Rome. The Jewish cemetery in Bad Rappenau near Heinschein is one of the largest in Germany. The oldest still-accessible gravestone dates from 1598; the last person was buried there in 1937.

JEWISH CEMETERY

Light in a nearby clearing –
the little girls gallop like horses in file
around the fields of ripe cucumbers and melons
as the black stain wells up
suddenly it appears like the awful ghost
of a shadow
to hide
the sin that emerges
a ruined Jewish cemetery
covered by thorny brambles.
The countrymen harvest the melons
the machine collects the cucumbers
the girls gallop around the cemetery
the dead Jews sleep on thorns
deliberately forgotten by the living and the dead.

It is happening at Bad Rappenau:
some of the sons of Germany are
　　　　　being killed twice over.

Translated from the Italian by Peter Ualrig Kennedy

CIMITERO EBRAICO

Presso una clarière – luce
tra campi di cetrioli maturi e meloni
le belle cavallerizze al galoppo in promenade
spunta la macchia nera
spunta all'improvviso come spettro
d'ombra
tremendo
da nascondere
spunta la colpa
un cimitero ebraico accartocciato arrugginito
coperto da rovi spinati.

I contadini raccolgono i meloni
la falciatrice trincia i cetrioli
le ragazze galoppano intorno al cimitero
i morti ebrei dormono sulle spine
volontariamente dimenticati da vivi e da morti.

Succede a Bad Rappenau
che alcuni dei figli di Germania siano
due volte ancisi...

MARIELLA MEHR

Mehr, born in 1947, is Swiss Yenish. The Yenish are a Western European itinerant people. As a traveller, Mehr was a victim of the 'Kinder der Landstrasse' project – a government rule applied from the 1930s until the 1970s, under which 'children of the road' were taken from their parents and given to adoptive families against their will.

NO SEA LAY AT OUR FEET...

No sea lay at our feet,
on the contrary, we escaped it
by the skin of our teeth
(troubles don't come singly, they say)
as the steel sky bound us to its heart.

In vain, in the places of skulls
we wept for our mothers,
and covered dead children with almond blossom,
to warm them in their sleep, their long sleep.

In black nights we are sown as seed
only for the earth, in the
morning hours, to be swept free of us, the later-born.

While you sleep I will find you wild herbs and mint;
Look down, eye, I say to you,
and you must never look in their faces
when their hands turn to stone.

For this the wild herbs, the mint.
They will lie peaceful on your forehead
when the reapers come.

For all Roma, Sinti and Yenish,
for all Jewish women and men,
for yesterday's murdered and those of tomorrow.

> *Translated from the German by Jean Boase-Beier*

KEIN MEER LAG UNS ZU FÜSSEN...

Kein Meer lag uns zu Füßen,
im Gegenteil, wir sind ihm
mit knapper Not entgangen, als
uns – kein Unglück, sagt man, kommt allein –
der stählerne Himmel ans Herz fesselte.

Umsonst haben wir an den Schädelstätten
um unsere Mütter geweint,
und tote Kinder mit Mandelblüten bedeckt,
sie zu wärmen im Schlaf, dem langen.

In schwarzen Nächten sät man uns aus
um dann, in den Morgenstunden,
die Erde von uns Nachgeborenen leerzufegen.

Noch im Schlaf such' ich Dir Wildkraut und Minze;
Fall ab, Auge, sage ich zu Dir,
und daß Du nie in ihre Gesichter sehen sollst,
wenn ihre Hände zu Stein werden.

Darum das Wildkraut, die Minze.
Sie liegen Dir still auf der Stirn,
wenn die Mäher kommen.

Für alle Roma, Sinti und Jenischen,
für alle Jüdinnen und Juden,
für die Ermordeten von gestern und die von morgen.

VOLKER VON TÖRNE

*Von Törne, born in 1934 in Quedlinburg (in Saxony-Anhalt, Germany),
was the son of an SS officer, and was tormented by guilt all his life as
a result. The poet was a director of 'Action Reconciliation – Service for
Peace', an international organisation that works to achieve reconstruction
and education in areas affected by fascism. He died in 1980.*

BIRKENAU

Here
no path goes
back

here
you remain
alone

with the beat
of your heart

with the ash
beneath the grass

here
words
end

Translated from the German by Jean Boase-Beier

BIRKENAU

Hier
führt kein Weg
zurück

hier
bleibst du
allein

mit dem Schlag
deines Herzens

mit der Asche
unter dem Gras

hier
enden
die Worte

OJĀRS VĀCIETIS

Rumbula is a forest near Riga, where 25,000 Jews were killed and buried on just two days: 30 November and 8 December, 1941. Vācietis, one of Latvia's most important twentieth-century poets, wrote this poem in 1964. He died in Riga in 1983 at the age of fifty.

RUMBULA

I pass the forest's eyes:
Against my shoulder rustle
The eyelashes of pines,
Beneath my feet sighs a soft mound of earth.

These are the only sounds;
I stop,
So there will be none.

Riven by my gaze,
The dam
No longer holds.

The forest is full of cries,
The forest is full of cries.

Cries
Frozen against the pines,
Cries
From the ragged bark.

Cries
From the earth
Over those buried alive,
From the mounds that did not grow still
Until dawn.

My racing pulse fells
This forest –
In the name of birches that tomorrow will grow,
In the name of children who tomorrow will live,
In the name of voices that won't cry out,
In the name of words that refuse to die.
And I shout
Into the forest's face,
– You! We don't need you now!

The forest, like a green crater,
Encircles me,
A green, angry voice
Passes through me like a current:
– Before my eyes
Thou shalt not promenade!
My lashes
Thou shalt not desire!
In my mounds,
Thou shalt not seek solace!

So no forest in the world
Should follow it,
I stand in Rumbula like a cry,
In a green crater of horror
Amidst the fields of grain.

All who enter me
Become my tongue,
My flame.
You who enter me –
Cry out!

Translated from the Latvian by Bitite Vinklers

RUMBULA

Mežam es gar pašām acīm eju,
Priežu skropstas man gar plecu švīkst,
Nopūšas zem kājām cinis mīksts . . .

Tās ir vienīgās skaņas,
Un es apstājos,
Lai nav nevienas.

Un vairs nevar apturēt
Dambi,
Ko pārrāvis skatiens.

Kliedzienu pilns mežs,
Kliedzienu pilns mežs.

Kliedz
Uz priežu stumbriem sastingušie
Šermuļi –
Šausmās raupja padarītā
Miza.

Kliedz
Virs dzīviem apraktajiem bērtie
Uzkalni –
Vēl līdz rītam kustējušies
Ciņi.

Pulss man dauzās
Un šo mežu cērt –
Bērzu vārdā, kuri parīt augs,
Bērnu vārdā, kuri parīt nāks,
Lūpu vārdā, kuras negrib kliegt,
Vārdu vārdā, kuri negrib mirt.
Un es mežam sejā
Tagad pats jau kliedzu:
– Tāda tevis šodien nevajaga! –
Kā zaļš krāteris mežs mani apņem,
Zaļa, nikna balss
Kā strāva iet caur mani:
– Tev gar manām acīm
Nebūs promenādēt!
Tev gar manām skropstām
Nebūs tīksmināties!
Tev ar maniem ciņiem
Nebūs mierināties! –

Lai nav visi zemes meži tādi,
Es te stāvu Rumbulā kā kliedziens,
Zaļgans šausmu krāteris starp druvām.

Katrs, kas ir manī kāju spēris,
Kļūst par manu mēli,
Manu liesmu.
Esi manī ienācis –
Un kliedz!

STEFAN HERTMANS

This poem by Hertmans (born in 1951 in Ghent) imagines the killings in Bosnia that started with the Nazi invasion in April 1941, helped by the Croatian fascist organisation Ustashe. Groups targeted for persecution were Jews, Roma and Serbs.

ICE-HOLES

When someone in Sarajevo had hit
target, the first tracks became
visible of a barren and desolate land,
half-forested still –

pine trees mainly, curled-up rails,
barbed-wire barriers, boots,
trampled faces and an endless
well in which maimed limbs like
half, uncomprehended letters disappeared,
that well of Arcimboldo,
without echo;
it took half a century
before each wound found a body.

A cruel cold surrounds us;
we have little chance of bail;
announced in the blood-red sun is
another night of staggering
frost, so that stone and star are
part of a same lifeless universe
that starts in fields and canals.

Voices and chunks rarely want to
get back together; an arm still drifts,
writes a spell in the snow,
while an eye clucks high somewhere,
higher than a guinea fowl on the chopping block.

It is a deep-brown eye, certainly
not aryan and not so sharp either,
more something like a shallow pond full of sand,
and with that frightening dark tone
as in the summer suddenly a shadow
falls over rippling water,
a new space, a new ice age
in a breathless and bleeding hole.

Translated from the Dutch by Marian de Vooght

WAKKEN

Toen iemand in Serajewo raak
geschoten had, werden de eerste wissels
zichtbaar van een bar en troosteloos gebied,
nog half bebost –

pijnbomen vooral, opgekrulde rails,
draadversperringen, laarzen,
getrapte gezichten en een onmetelijke
put waarin verminkte ledematen als
halve, onbegrepen letters verdwenen,
die put van Arcimboldo,
zonder echo;
het duurde een halve eeuw
voor iedere wond een lichaam vond.

Een wrede kou omgeeft ons;
op borgsommen hebben we weinig kans;
in de bloedrode zon kondigt zich
andermaal een nacht aan van duizelingwekkend
vriezen, zodat steen en ster tot
een zelfde levenloos heelal behoren
dat in akkers en grachten begint.

Stemmen en hompen willen elkaar
maar zelden terug; een arm zwerft nog,
schrijft een bezwering in de sneeuw,

terwijl een oog ergens hoog klokt,
hoger dan een parelhoen op het kapblok.

Het is een diepbruin oog, ongetwijfeld
niet arisch en verder ook niet zo scherp,
meer zoiets als een ondiepe vijver vol zand,
en met die angstwekkende donkere toon
als in de zomer plots een schaduw
over rimpelend water valt,
een nieuwe ruimte, een nieuwe ijstijd
in een ademloos en bloedend wak.

NITSA DORI

Dori, who was born in 1960 in Haifa, is a specialist in Sephardic studies. Her parents emigrated from Istanbul to Israel in 1948.

IF I DID NOT BELIEVE IN YOU...

If I did not believe in you
I would not be writing you these words,
I am writing in the firm belief
these words of mine by you are heard.
A commandment you gave us,
forbidding us to kill:
in the camps you might have saved us
but you left us to be killed,
and your mercy,
your mercy, where was it
while a young child burned to death?

If it's vengeance that you seek
for your people once again,
I pray:
let the little ones, the weak,
let them be saved.

Translated from the Ladino by Anna Crowe

SI EN TI NO ME CREÍA...

Si en ti no me creía
esta letra a ti no te escribía,
con grande creencia la estó escribiendo
que mis palabras estás sintiendo.
Una comandamienta mos dates,
mos dates de no matar
y tú en los campos dejates,
dejates matar sin apartar
y tu piadad,
tu piadad, ¿ánde estaba
cuando un beibico se quemaba?

Si venganza es que quieres
otra vez de tu pueblo tomar,
te rogo:
ia los chicos déjalos,
déjalos salvar!

DAVID FRAM

Fram was born in Ponevezh, Lithuania, in 1903. In this poem, Zion refers to South Africa, where he emigrated in 1927. Fram, who died in Johannesburg in 1988, was a strong opponent of racism and apartheid.

AN ANSWER TO THE WORLD

I feel I wear the yellow star again.
The smoke balls out of the limekiln far away,
Where my dad lived out his final Shema
Where my mum breathed out her final breath.

Where brothers went resignedly to death
Where infants took their silent wobbling steps
Wrapped in a heart-warming motherly song
So they did not cry before dying – O my God!...

And I can see still today, can still feel the hell
Of those times not so very long ago
When the lightest punishment was: burn him
That was the sentence – the executioner's black call

They killed us and choked us without let
The greater the murder the gladder they felt
The bright gleam of morning did not stop them
The most horrible cry did not stop them…

And so the Jews went to the pyre
From Warsaw and Paris, from Kaunas and Bonn.
Millions trekked on and on and on
To the black place of execution – six million all told!…

The whole world looked on and said not a word
Stood unmoved with their hands at their sides,
And the dead they left in great piles to lie
Burned them one by one, slaughtered and burned…

Until a wonder redeemed us, and set us free,
There appeared to us an outstretched hand.
With hope, with trust, with revitalised dreams
It led us right back to our own land.

Those who had hidden in villages and towns,
Who'd managed to avoid the murdering sword
With pious prayers went proudly out
Saved from death – they stayed in our land.

And here it happened – they began to build
Each just wanted to live happy and free
The earth grew wet, fruited by the dew
That was tapped by every flower and tree.

A people came alive, ploughers and sowers,
They tended sheep, they cut their bread
And Jews from afar, like desert travellers –
Began to conquer their fear of death.

This is now their home, they will protect it
As heroes they are ready with their sweat and their blood
And if there is thunder and burning and flashing –
No-one will ever rein in their courage

The peaceful fields have begun to bloom
With overwhelming light the day is come
The light of life, the radiance of Zion,
Our wound is healed, our lament is stilled.

This we felt, this we understood:
The fig tree will grow in peace at your door.
Here we will stay, go away no more
We will never move out of this place again.

The remnant of a people, the final survivors
Will grow here again, a balm to the wound...
And the heavens above looked upon us in joy
With sabbath-like peace after the week's hard toil...

Translated from the Yiddish by Jean Boase-Beier & Marian de Vooght

AN ENTFER DER VELT

Ikh fil, ikh trog oyf zikh tsurik di gele late.
Fun vaytn knoylt zikh nokh fun kalkh-oyvn der roykh,
Vu s'hot zayn letstn Shma Yisroel oysgelebt mayn tate,
Vu s'hot mayn mame oysgehoykht ir letstn hoykh,

Vu brider zaynen tsu dem toyt farlitene gegangen,
Vu oyfhelekh geshtelt hobn in vakl zeyer shtiln trot,
Farviklte in hartsike, in mameshe gezangn,
Zey zoln farn shtarbn khotsh nit veynen – o mayn Got!...

Un kh'ze nokh haynt un fil nokh dem gehenem
Fun gornisht-lang fargangenem amol,
Ven laykhtste shtrof gevezn iz: – 'farbren im',
Dos iz der psak – dem henkers shvartser kol –

Hot men keseyder unz geharget un gevorgn, –
Vos greser s'iz der mord – alts freylikher iz zey.
Es hot zey nit geshtert di hele shayn fun morgn,
Es hot zey nit geshtilt der groylikster geshrey...

Azoy zaynen gegangn yidn tsu dem shayter –
Fun Varshe un Pariz, fun Kovne un fun Bon.
Milyonen hobn zikh getsoygn vayter, vayter
Tsum shvartsn eshafot... oy, gantse zeks milyon!...

Oyf dem – di gantse velt gekukt hot un geshvign,
Geshtanen glaykhgiltik mit aropgelozte hent,
Un meysim kupesvayz hot men gelozn lign
Un nokhanand gebrent, geshokhtn un gebrent…

Biz vanen s'hot a nes unz oysgeleyzt, bafrayte,
Es hot bavizn zikh an oysgeshtrekte hant.
Mit hofn un mit treyst, mit zeungen banayte
Zi hot unz drayst gefirt tsurik tsu unzer land.

Di oysbahaltene in derfer un in shtetlekh,
Vos oysgehit zey hobn zikh fun merderisher shverd –
Gegangen zaynen shtolts mit tfiles frum un getlekh
Geratevet fun toyt – bazetsn unzer erd.

Un do iz dos geshen – men hot genumen boyen,
S'hot yederer gevolt zikh oyslebn in freyd…
S'iz erd gevorn faykht, bafrukhpert fun di toyen,
Vos ayngezapt hot zat do yeder boym un kveyt.

S'hot oyfgelebt a folk fun akerer un zeyer,
Men hot gepashet shof, men hot geshnitn broyt
Un yidn fun der vayt, vi durkhn midber-geyer –
Zikh oyfgehert tsu shrekn hobn farn toyt.

Dos iz dokh zeyer heym, zey veln zikh bashitsn,
Vi heldn zaynen greyt – mit zeyer shveys un blut
Un zol es dunern un flakern un blitsn –
S'vet keyner ayntsoymen nit kenen zeyer mut…

Di felder fridlekhe genumen hobn blien,
Mit groyser likhtikeyt gekumen iz der tog,
Di likhtikeyt fun zayn, di oysshtralung fun Tsien,
Geheylt hot unzer vund, geshtilt hot unzer klog…

Azoy hot men gefilt, azoy hot men farshtanen:
Der faygnboym in ru vet vaksn bay dayn tir.
Men vet shoyn blaybn do, men vet nit geyn fun danen,
Men vet zikh funem ort atsind nit ton keyn rir.

Di reshtlekh fun a folk, der iberblayb fun pleyte
Vet opvaksn tsurik un lindern dem brokh…
Un himlen iber unz gekukt hobn derfreyte
Mit shabesdiker ru oyf pratse fun der vokh…

FLORY JAGODA

Born in Sarajevo in 1926, Jagoda is one of the very few Bosnian Jews who survived the Holocaust. She has lived in America since 1946, and is a singer-songwriter, dedicated to preserving Sephardic folk songs.

THEY ALL WENT

The alleyways and lanes are empty,
in the houses no balsam grows,
no pots of roses at the windows,
no clove-pinks, sisters in their beauty.
The orchards are without their lovers,
no grannies, hair coiled in a bun,
and the cradles where the mothers
sat and sang to a little one.
Where did they go?
Where did they go?
Where did they go?
All, all, they all went,
all of them, all, they all went.

And the rabbis who read to us from the Torah
the prayers that bestowed on us their peace,
and our children's joyful weddings
where we danced as we played the tambourine
and the cradles where the mothers
sat and sang to a little one.
Where did they go?
Where did they go?
Where did they go?
All, all, they all went,
all of them, all, they all went.

Translated from the Ladino by Anna Crowe

TODOS SI JUERON

Las calejas son vaciyas,
las casas son sin alegriyas,
las ventanas son sin rosas,
caránfilis cunjás hermosas,
las guartas son sin enamuradus,

nu hay más nonas cun tucadus
y las mujeris cun las cunas
que cantaban a las criyaturas.
¿Ónde si jueron?,
¿ónde si jueron?,
¿ónde si jueron?
Todos, todos si jueron,
todos, todos si jueron.

Y lus jajamís que mus maldaban
las oraciones que paz mus daban
y las bodas de lus fijicus
que mus bailaban cun lus pandericus
y las madris cun las cunas
que cantaban a sus criyaturas.
¿Ónde si jueron?,
¿ónde si jueron?,
¿ónde si jueron?
Todos, todos si jueron,
todos, todos si jueron.

SAUL VAN MESSEL

After the deportation of their inhabitants, the houses in Amsterdam's poorest Jewish neighbourhood around Waterloo Square were demolished and the area was redeveloped in the 1970s. Also see the information for van Messel's poem 'sign', p. 178.

URBAN RENEWAL / AUTUMN 1977

homesickness:
the lining
of my thought

visible
when the wind
catches my words

Translated from the Dutch by David Colmer

GESANEERD / HERFST 1977

heimwee:
de voering
van mijn geheugen

zichtbaar
als de wind
mijn woorden opwaait

IDA GERHARDT

Gerhardt suffered lifelong regret for having signed, under pressure, an Aryan declaration in 1941 to keep her job as a classics teacher. Also see the note for her poem 'The Rejected Gift', p. 136.

INSCRIPTION IN STONE

This is the procession of the Jews, with ropes they are bound,
on the table of rock their naked soles stand;
the men struck silent, the women overburdened
with children clutching their fastened hands.

Pharaoh's deed is written in the granite;
proud hieroglyphs tell of number and tribe.
I see a grim platform, the Jews arrested,
the eyes looking left, as Pharaoh required.

A single mistake would cost the mason his life:
no name should be absent from the train of slaves.
To ensure *they* would go, with my pen I wrote
carving the letters that can never be erased.

Translated from the Dutch by Marian de Vooght

STEEN-INSCRIPTIE

Dit is de stoet der Joden, saamgesnoerd met touwen,
de blote zolen op het rotsplateau geplant;
de mannen stom gefnuikt, de lastbeladen vrouwen
met kinderen geklemd aan de gebonden hand.

De daad van Pharaoh in het graniet geschreven;
trotse hiëroglyphen melden stam en tal.
Ik zie een grauw perron, de Joden saamgedreven,
de rijen ogen links, naar Pharaoh beval.

De steenhouwer zou één fout met de dood bekopen:
er mag geen naam ontbreken in de slaventrein.
Opdat zij zouden gaan, schroefde ik de schrijfstift open,
de letters zettend die nooit uit te wissen zijn.

JACQUES ROZENBERG

Rozenberg was born in 1922 in Poland. He was sent to Dosselin prison in Mechlin for being in the Belgian Resistance, and subsequently deported to Auschwitz. Although trained as a violinist, he became a painter and writer after the war. He died in Brussels in 1999.

PAIN. REVOLT. HOPE. LIFE AFTER THE EVENT...

Having been entrained for death, how to retrain for life?
A whole past life to surmount, to conquer!
Act as if.
Act as if you're the same as everyone else.
The ones who didn't go through it.

Trains now were just for taking our problems from place to place.

Back in the world of civilisation,
Or civil lies and violation,
We were the flotsam of dreams of brotherhood and peace,
But few took any interest in us,
In our state of mind, or even body.

We were left to our own devices.
No reception centres,
No squads of doctors or psychologists
To listen and help.

Trains now were just for getting away, no matter where.
Headlong away
To escape
The useless toings and froings
And then back again.

Translated from the French by Ian Higgins

DOULEURS. RÉVOLTES. ESPOIRS. LA VIE APRÈS...

Comment faire d'un train de mort un train de vie ?
Tout ce passé, il a fallu le surmonter, le vaincre.
Faire comme si.
Faire comme si l'on est semblable aux autres.
Ceux qui ne l'ont pas vécu.

Les trains n'ont plus alors servi qu'à déplacer nos problèmes.

Rendus à la vie dite civile,
Souvent si vile,
Par les rêves de fraternité et de paix, détruits,
Peu de personnes se sont préoccupées de nous,
De notre état psychologique même pas physiologique.

Nous avons été laissés à nous-mêmes.
Pas de cellule d'accueil,
Pas d'escouades de médecins, de psychologues,
Pour nous écouter, nous aider.

Les trains n'ont plus alors servi qu'à rejoindre des ailleurs.
Fuites en avant
Pour échapper
Aux travers de multiples passages
Où arriver à nouveau.

BERT VOETEN

*The first lines of Voeten's poem 'De trein' form the motto of the famous
Holocaust novella* Het bittere kruid *(Bitter Herbs) by Dutch writer
Marga Minco. Minco hid in Voeten's house during the war and married
him afterwards. All of Minco's family were deported and killed. Voeten
died in 1992.*

THE TRAIN

A train full of Jews is rolling
through my head. I change
the points of the past and count
the bolted cattle-trucks:
fifty trucks and in each truck
there's fifty people. Wedged
between limbs, everybody
on or under one another,
prisoners to each other
in the darkness of the wagon
in the darkness without water
without air
without hope.

It is seven hundred and fifty miles
to Sobibor – I worked it out
one evening with a map
of Europe on the table.
They didn't know, they only knew
the battens bruising their backbones,
their tongues swelling like blisters,
their eyes smarting, their feet dead
in their shoes; they learnt
that on the second or third day
you wet yourself, you use
your nails to make some room
when lying on the hard body
of someone who's suffocated.

Yesterday no longer seemed real,
the white tablecloth on Friday
evening, the lights of Hanukkah;

tomorrow was as yet unknown,
the undressing, the tiled rooms,
the waterless showerheads,
the eye that would watch.
They only knew this now
with its wooden cage, its darkness,
the now of the madness that comes
with screams and foaming mouths,
the now of the outside world:
a station in Nieder-Lausitz, the smell
of onion soup, Schweinebraten,
the patter of fresh water,
boots on gravel, a voice from
an iron throat and the butt
of a rifle, pounding on
the outside boards.

*

'They should have gassed
them all,' someone said recently
on a train in this low country.
It was a salesman in an over-heated
second-class smoking compartment –
they had to open the window.

Another train went rolling
through my head when I read about it,
a train full of Jews. I counted
the bolted cattle-trucks:
fifty trucks,
fifty people in each truck;
prisoners to each other
in the dark wooden cage
in the madness of this world.

Translated from the Dutch by David Colmer

DE TREIN

Er rijdt door mijn hoofd een trein
vol joden, ik leg het verleden
als een wissel om en ik tel
de veewagons met de grendels:
vijftig wagons, in elke
wagon vijftig mensen. Men ligt
geklemd tussen ledematen,
men is drager of gedragene,
gevangenen van elkander
in het duister van de wagon
in het duister zonder water,
zonder lucht,
zonder hoop.

Het is twaalfhonderd kilometer
naar sobibor – ik heb het
op een avond uitgerekend
met een kaart van europa voor me.
Zíj wisten het niet, zij wisten
alleen dat hun wervels kneusden
tegen de baddings, hun tong
zwol als een blaar, hun ogen
schrijnden, hun voeten dood
in hun schoenen staken; zij leerden
dat men na twee, drie dagen
zijn water laat lopen, zijn nagels
gebruikt om ruimte te krijgen
wanneer men ligt op het harde
lichaam van een gestikte.

Niemand wist meer van gisteren,
van het witte tafellaken
op vrijdagavond, de lichtjes
van chanoeka; niemand wist nog
van morgen, van de ontkleding,
de betegelde douchelokalen,
de sproeidoppen zonder water,
het oog dat hen gade zou slaan.
Men kende alleen het nu
van de houten kooi, van het donker,
het nu van de waanzin die komt
met mondschuim en gillen, het nu
van de wereld buiten: een halte
in nieder-lausitz, de geur van
uiensoep, schweinebraten,

het kletteren van vers water,
laarzen op grint, een stem uit
een ijzeren keel, en beukend
tegen het wandbeschot de
grondpaat van een geweer.

*

'Ze hadden ze allemááál
in de gaskamer moeten stoppen'
heeft onlangs iemand gezegd
in een trein in dit platte land.
Het was een koopman, hij zat
in een 2e klas rookcoupé
met een al te hete verwarming –
het raampje moest er bij open.

Er reed een andere trein door
mijn hoofd toen ik dit las,
een trein vol joden. Ik telde
de veewagons met de grendels:
vijftig wagons,
in elke wagon vijftig mensen;
gevangenen van elkander
in de duistere houten kooi
in de waanzin van deze wereld.

NINA KOKKALIDOU NAHMIA

*Thessaloniki writer Kokkalidou Nahmia (1920-2002) remembered the fate
of her Jewish fellow citizens in many of her poems and stories.*

THEM AND US

Now that the day's wages are balanced
with the percentage of our conscience,
it's pointless to chase our shadows
that didn't shade those marked for death
our human tears
that didn't extinguish the burning ovens
the poison of our revolution
that wasn't stronger than the gas.

Now that our footsteps resound in the streets
it's pointless to observe how many stones there are
and to search for the traces
of children's feet in the snow.

Let's unearth the sacred *taleth*
hidden in the imperishable spirit,
and let's weave their ashes
into the fringes.

As for us now, let's journey into the wilderness.

Translated from the Greek by David Connolly

ΕΚΕΊΝΟΙ ΚΙ ΕΜΕΊΣ

Τώρα που τα μεροκάματα ισοζυγιάστηκαν
με το ποσοστό της συνείδησής μας,
είναι μάταιο να κυνηγάμε τη σκιά μας
που δεν δρόσισε τους προγραμματισμένους στο χαμό
τ' ανθρώπινα δάκρυά μας
που δεν έσβησαν τ' αναμμένα καμίνια
το δηλητήριο της επανάστασής μας
που δεν ήταν δυνατότερο απ' τ' αέριο.

Τώρα που τα βήματά μας αντηχούν στους δρόμους
είναι μάταιο να παρατηρούμε πόσες πέτρες υπάρχουν
και να ψάχνουμε για τ' αχνάρια
των παιδικών ποδιών πάνω στα χιόνια.

Ας ξεθάψουμε τα ιερά ταλέθ,
κρυμμένα στο άφθαρτο πνεύμα,
κι ας πλέξουμε στα κρόσια τους
τη στάχτη εκείνων.

Εμείς τώρα ας πορευτούμε προς την έρημο.

STANISLAV SMELYANSKY

As a Jewish writer and musician, Smelyansky is dedicated to producing Holocaust-related work that creates awareness in the next generations. Also see the note for Smelyansky's poem 'Dancing Gypsy', p. 102.

GUILTY!

Quiet anger, fury –
Where is my beloved people?
The world accused fascists –
I accuse the world.

I can't gag myself –
keep wheezing about the wrong.
You say: 'Gestapo!'
I accuse you – all.

Kaddish, prayer, mass –
Six million times.
You accused Hess –
Now look at yourself!

Heroes won't save
Those they liberated.
For this crime
Will the Day of Reckoning come ?

Cursed generation –
You horde of subhumans.
For this crime
I consign you to perdition
Forever.

Translated from the Russian by Veronika Krasnova

ВИНОВНЫ

Тихий мой гнев неистов.
Где мой народ-кумир?
Мир обвинил фашистов.
Я обвиняю мир.

В рот не засунешь кляпа:
Буду хрипеть про грех.
Все говорят: 'Гестапо!'
Я обвиняю – всех.

Каддиш, молебен, месса –
Шесть миллионов раз.
Вы обвинили Гесса.
Я обвиняю вас.

Тех, кто обрел свободу –
Подвиги не спасут.
За приговор народу
Будет ли Страшный Суд?

Проклято поколенье.
Полулюдей орда.
Проклято – Преступленье.
Проклято. Навсегда.

HUGUES C. PERNATH

Belgian poet Pernath was born in 1931. His visit to Łódź and Auschwitz in 1967 had an enormous impact on him and his writing. In 1970 he married Myra Vecht, who had been imprisoned as a child with her parents in Terezín. Pernath died in 1975.

LIKE NOTHING. OR LIKE THE FALTERING OF TIME...

Like nothing. Or like the faltering of time
Classifies death and suddenly and out of the blue
The slow shadow of my solitude became my riches.
I knew the cargos, the stubbles in the straw,
The truth that made my earlier love
My life before, sink
To mould and mud.
Turning my faith, my unrest
To remorse and rot.

Everybody must know this, everybody
Whether only the fire, or only the gas
For as I protest, for as I perish I recognise your race.

Jacob, your corpses fell in a desert,
Doubt, but on this ground I have sworn
That she shall remain after that hail,
That I will carry her like a tree.
And of you, Sarah-Rose, I beg your blessing for me,
For her, your daughter, and for all people
Out of whom children live that give offense.
Joy that paralyzes.

Translated from the Dutch by Marian de Vooght

ZOALS NIETS. OF ZOALS HET HAPEREN VAN DE TIJD...

Zoals niets. Of zoals het haperen van de tijd
De dood rangschikt en plots en onverwacht
De trage schaduw van de eenzaamheid mijn weelde werd.
Ik kende de vrachten, de stoppels in het stro,
De waarheid die de vroegere liefde
Mijn leven voordien, verlaagde
Tot schimmel en schoor.
Mijn overtuiging, mijn onrust verbuigend
Tot wroeging en verval.

Iedereen moet dit weten, iedereen
Of alleen het vuur, of alleen het gas
Want steigerend, want stervend herken ik jouw ras.

Jacob, jullie lijken vielen in een woestijn,
Twijfel, maar op deze grond heb ik gezworen
Dat zij zal overblijven na de hagel,
Dat ik haar zal dragen als een boom.
En van jou, Sarah-Rose, smeek ik jouw zegen voor mij,
Voor haar, jouw dochter, en voor alle mensen
Waaruit kinderen leven die aanstoot geven.
Vreugde die verlamt.

IBOJA WANDALL-HOLM

See the note for Wandall-Holm's poem 'Field Work in Auschwitz', p. 62.

TWENTY MINUTES TO TWELVE

Abracadabra. Angola. Astronaut. Barcelona. Congo.
Dallas. Gas.
The thoughts appear in alphabetical order.
Stop at M and N. Melancholy nocturne. Nature
morte. Never more.
Magnate. Master. Massacre. Mass-deceit. Militarism.
Megadeath.
Mauthausen.
Never sane. Neck shot. Nationalism. Nazism. Napalm.
Neuengamme.
Night.

Translated from the Danish by Marian de Vooght

TYVE MINUTTER I TOLV

Abrakadabra. Angola. Astronaut. Barcelona. Congo.
Dallas. Gas.
Tankerne kommer i alfabetisk rækkefølge.
Standser ved M og N. Melankolsk nocturne. Nature
morte. Never more.
Magnat. Magt. Massakre. Maskepi. Militarisme.
Megadeath.
Mauthausen.
Narreværk. Nakkeskud. Nationalisme. Nazisme. Napalm.
Neuengamme.
Nat.

BORIS SLUTSKY

Slutsky, a Russian Jewish poet, was born in Ukraine in 1919. He served as a political commissar in the Soviet army from 1941 to 1945. In many of his poems, Slutsky displayed Soviet discourse and stripped it of ideological meaning. He died in 1986.

I OFTEN DREAM OF AUSCHWITZ NOWADAYS...

I often dream of Auschwitz nowadays,
the road between the station and the barracks.
One of the crowd, I walk like some poor Lazarus,
my suitcase hammering against my back.

I'd probably predicted what would be,
and found a small one, fairly light and handy.
I'm in that crowd, dressed lightly, for the weekend.
Surveying my surroundings as I walk.

Others had bigger cases, bundles too,
to carry with them,
                    even bales, and boxes,
stacked high as villages up in the mountains.
And carrying those bales was something hard.

A journey through a dream is longer far
than the real thing, it's tougher, more protracted.
As if instead of walking, now you're swimming,
and every stroke's more feeble and more slow.

One of the crowd, I hurry but I don't,
my heart congealed, my heart no longer beating.
My soul had frozen long before and couldn't
recover any warmth along that road.

A factory plain of purpose issued forth
its vile sweet smoke
                    as if in greeting to us,
that vile smoke, flying heavy,
                    like a swan does,
tormented what we still had of our souls.

Translated from the Russian by Gerry Smith

ТЕПЕРЬ ОСВЕНЦИМ ЧАСТО СНИТСЯ МНЕ...

Теперь Освенцим часто снится мне:
дорога между станцией и лагерем.
Иду, бреду с толпою бедным Лазарем,
а чемодан колотит по спине.

Наверно, что-то я подозревал
и взял удобный, легкий чемоданчик.
Я шел с толпою налегке, как дачник.
Шел и окрестности обозревал.

А люди чемоданы и узлы
несли с собой,
                        и кофры, и баулы,
высокие, как горные аулы.
Им были те баулы тяжелы.

Дорога через сон куда длинней,
чем наяву, и тягостней и длительней.
Как будто не идешь – плывешь по ней,
и каждый взмах все тише и медлительней.

Иду как все: спеша и не спеша,
и не стучит застынувшее сердце.
Давным-давно замерзшая душа
на том шоссе не сможет отогреться.

Нехитрая промышленность дымит
навстречу нам
                        поганым сладким дымом,
 и медленным полетом
                                лебединым
остатки душ поганый дым томит.

DAN PAGIS

Pagis was born in 1930 in the German-speaking region of Bukovina in Romania. He survived a concentration camp in Transnistria and emigrated to Palestine in 1946, becoming a scholar of mediaeval Hebrew literature, and writing his poetry in Hebrew. He died in 1986 in Jerusalem.

TESTIMONY

No, no, they were definitely
human: uniforms, boots,
how to say it? They were made
in the image.

I was a shadow.
I had a different maker.

And He in His grace hasn't left in me
anything that could perish.
And I ran to him, I ascended,
light, bluish, reconciled,
I'd say, apologetic:
smoke to almighty smoke
of no face or figure.

Translated from the Hebrew by Tsipi Keller

עֵדוּת

לֹא לֹא: הֵם בְּהֶחְלֵט
הָיוּ בְּנֵי אָדָם: מַדִּים, מַגָּפַיִם.
אֵיךְ לְהַסְבִּיר. הֵם נִבְרְאוּ בְּצֶלֶם.

אֲנִי הָיִיתִי צֵל.
לִי הָיָה בּוֹרֵא אַחֵר.

וְהוּא בְּחַסְדּוֹ לֹא הִשְׁאִיר בִּי מַה שֶׁיָּמוּת.
וּבָרַחְתִּי אֵלָיו, עָלִיתִי קַלִּיל, כָּחֹל,
מְפַיֵּס, הָיִיתִי אוֹמֵר: מִתְנַצֵּל:
עָשָׁן אֶל עָשָׁן כָּל יָכוֹל
שֶׁאֵין לוֹ גּוּף וּדְמוּת.

SAUL VAN MESSEL

Van Messel started writing poetry only in 1967. All of his poems are concerned with being Jewish, and often register a struggle with what it means to be a Jew after having survived the Holocaust. Also see the information for van Messel's poem 'sign', p. 178.

WHAT A COINCIDENCE

last night i saw
jews running away /
how could they know
that i was dreaming
of a roundup

Translated from the Dutch by David Colmer

OOK TOEVALLIG

vannacht zag ik
joden weghollen /
hoe zouden zij weten
dat ik van een
razzia droomde

YAEL GLOBERMAN

A poet, writer of fiction and literary translator (from English into Hebrew), Globerman was born in Tel Aviv in 1959. Her parents survived the Holocaust in Poland.

SECOND GENERATION

The man who almost wasn't sits down at the table.
The woman who barely made it serves him plum cake.
This is my home: It is good here. Safe.
Mother leans on Father. Father leans on a shadow.
At night they tiptoe into my room in beekeepers' suits,
rub my temples with wax.
We are a very warm family.
The floor burns under our feet.

We believe in walls. Believe less in a roof.
It has to be built every morning anew. We build.
There is ammunition in the medicine cabinet
and a bribe in the bank for the guard
who lets us steal across the border every night.
Silence is the pitch that stops up gaps, seals the floors.
I hear something deep roaring and surging:
There's a sea underneath the foundations of home.

*

This house is filled with love. Father is strong
and mother good-looking.
Gershwin could have written our lullaby.
What good will this sorrow do
Where will I lead this sorrow
Where will I sit it down when it gets here
What will I give it to eat

Translated from the Hebrew by Vivian Eden

דור שני

הָאִישׁ שֶׁכְּמְעַט לֹא הָיָה יוֹשֵׁב לַשֻּׁלְחָן.
הָאִשָּׁה שֶׁבְּקֹשִׁי הִגִּיעָה מַגִּישָׁה לוֹ עוּגַת שְׁזִיפִים.
זֶה הַבַּיִת שֶׁלִּי: טוֹב פֹּה. בָּטוּחַ.
אִמָּא נִשְׁעֶנֶת עַל אַבָּא. אַבָּא נִשְׁעָן עַל צֵל.
בַּלַּיְלָה הֵם פּוֹסְעִים לְחַדְרֵי עַל קְצוֹת אֶצְבָּעוֹת
בְּתִלְבֹּשֶׁת כּוֹרְנִים, מוֹשְׁחִים אֶת רְקוֹתַי בְּשַׁעֲוָה.
אֲנַחְנוּ מִשְׁפָּחָה מְאֹד חַמָּה.
הָרִצְפָּה בּוֹעֶרֶת מִתַּחַת לַרַגְלַיִם.

אֲנַחְנוּ מַאֲמִינִים בַּקִּירוֹת. פָּחוֹת מַאֲמִינִים בַּגַּג.
צָרִיךְ לִבְנוֹת אוֹתוֹ כָּל בֹּקֶר מֵחָדָשׁ. אֲנַחְנוּ בּוֹנִים.
בְּאָרוֹן הַתְּרוּפוֹת יֵשׁ תַּחְמֹשֶׁת וּבַבַּנְק שֹׁחַד לַשּׁוֹמֵר
שֶׁמַּעֲבִיר אוֹתָנוּ, לַיְלָה לַיְלָה, אֶת הַגְּבוּל.
שְׁתִּיקָה הִיא הַגֹּפֶר שֶׁסּוֹתֵם אֶת הַפְּרָצוֹת, אוֹטֵם אֶת הָרִצְפָּה.
אֲנִי שׁוֹמַעַת מַשֶּׁהוּ עָמֹק נוֹהֵם:
יָם קַיָּם מִתַּחַת לִיסוֹדוֹת הַבַּיִת.

*

הַבַּיִת הַזֶּה מָלֵא אַהֲבָה. אַבָּא חָזָק וְאִמָּא יָפָה.
גֶּרְשְׁוִין הָיָה יָכוֹל לִכְתֹּב עָלֵינוּ שִׁיר עֶרֶשׂ.
מַה יַּעֲזֹר הַצַּעַר הַזֶּה
לְאָן לְהוֹלִיךְ אֶת הַצַּעַר הַזֶּה
אֵיפֹה אוֹשִׁיב אוֹתוֹ כְּשֶׁיַּגִּיעַ
מָה אֶתֵּן לוֹ לֶאֱכֹל

NINA KOKKALIDOU NAHMIA

See the note for Kokkalidou Nahmia's poem 'Them and Us', p. 207.

AFTER TWENTY YEARS IN AUSCHWITZ

You said to me: I'll travel,
I'll sleep, open the window,
born again I'll chatter,
I'll see the earth dug for my burial,
the same earth where bleeding I was dragged
into the closed wagons.
In my one hand I hold resurrection,
in my other eternal remembrance.

Translated from the Greek by David Connolly

ΜΕΤΑ ΕΊΚΟΣΙ ΧΡΟΝΙΑ ΣΤΟ ΆΟΥΣΒΙΤΣ

Μου είπες: Θα ταξιδέψω,
θα κοιμηθώ, θ' ανοίξω το παράθυρο,
θα κουβεντιάσω ξαναγεννημένη,
θα ιδώ τη γη που 'χαν ανασκάψει για την ταφή μου,
την ίδια γη που σύρθηκα αιμοστάζουσα
μέσα στο κλειστό βαγόνι.
Στό 'να μου χέρι κρατώ την ανάσταση,
στ' άλλο μου χέρι κρατώ την αιώνια μνήμη.

TUVIA RUEBNER

See the note for Ruebner's poem 'Testimony', p. 109.

A POSTCARD FROM PRESSBURG-BRATISLAVA

Bratislava is Pressburg is Pozsony.
For me it is Pressburg.
My teacher, Mr. Wurm from the elementary school,
pulled a class photo from his drawer and started pointing:
"This one was a Nazi, and this one and that one too. This one
was especially brutal. This one fell in Russia
and that one was deported. Which of the Jewish pupils
survived – I do not know."

Pressburg was a tri-lingual city. Its fourth language
is silence.
Were there once borders to evil?
Pressburg lies adjacent to the Danube, at the edges of the
    Carpathian slopes.
Near the Cathedral the Neologist Synagogue once stood
built in some kind of Moorish style. Below is Fish Square,
above is where the Street of the Jews began. The Danube flows
    as always.
I am old. I can walk only slowly now.
I was born in Pressburg. I had a mother, a father, a sister.
I had, I believe, a small and happy childhood in Pressburg.
Once, the Danube froze solid.
The Celts built here a fortress, as did the princes
of greater Moravia. The Romans called this place
Possonium. This is an old old city.
So old I barely know her anymore.
Farewell, beloved, it's unimaginable.

Translated from the Hebrew by Rachel Tzvia Back

גְּלוּיָה מִפְּרֶשְׁבּוּרְג־בְּרָטִיסְלָוָה

בְּרָטִיסְלָוָה הִיא פְּרֶשְׁבּוּרג הִיא פּוֹזוֹנִי.
בִּשְׁבִילִי הִיא פְּרֶשְׁבּוּרְג.
מוֹרִי, מַר וּוּרְם מֵהָעֲמָמִי
הוֹצִיא מִמְגֵרָתוֹ אֶת תַּצְלוּם הַכְּתָּה וְהִצְבִּיעַ:
זֶה הָיָה נָאצִי וְגַם זֶה וְזֶה. הַהוּא
הָיָה אַכְזָרִי בְּמְיֻחָד. הַלָּה נָפַל בְּרוּסְיָה
וְאוֹתוֹ גֵּרְשׁוּ. מִי מֵהַתַּלְמִידִים הַיְּהוּדִים
שָׂרַד וָחַי – אֵינִי יוֹדֵעַ.
פְּרֶשְׁבּוּרְג הָיְתָה עִיר תְּלַת־לְשׁוֹנִית. הַלָּשׁוֹן הָרְבִיעִית
הִיא הַשְּׁתִיקָה.
הַאִם הָיוּ פַּעַם גְּבוּלוֹת לָרַע?
פְּרֶשְׁבּוּרְג שׁוֹכֶנֶת לְיַד הַדָּנוּבָּה, בְּקְצֵה שְׁלוּחוֹת הַקַּרְפָּטִים.
בְּקִרְבַת הַקָּתֶדְרָלָה עָמַד בֵּית־הַכְּנֶסֶת שֶׁל הַנֵּיאוֹלוֹגִים
בְּסִגְנוֹן מָאוּרִי כָּלְשֶׁהוּ. לְמַטָּה שְׂרוּעָה כִּכַּר הַדָּגִים
לְמַעְלָה הִתְחִיל רְחוֹב הַיְּהוּדִים. הַדָּנוּבָּה זוֹרֶמֶת כְּמוֹ תָּמִיד.
אֲנִי זָקֵן. אֵינִי יָכוֹל לְהִתְקַדֵּם אֶלָּא לְאַט.
בִּפְרֶשְׁבּוּרְג נוֹלַדְתִּי. הָיוּ לִי אֵם, אָב וְאָחוֹת.
הָיְתָה לִי, כִּמְדֻמֶּה, יַלְדוּת קְטַנָּה מְאֻשֶּׁרֶת בִּפְרֶשְׁבּוּרְג.
פַּעַם קָפְאָה הַדָּנוּבָּה כָּל־כֻּלָּה.
הַקֶּלְטִים בָּנוּ כָּאן מִבְצָר, וְגַם נְסִיכֵי
מוֹרַבְיָה רַבָּתִי. הָרוֹמָאִים קָרְאוּ לַמָּקוֹם
פּוֹזוֹנְיּוּם. זֹאת עִיר בָּאָה־בַּיָּמִים.
כֹּה בָּאָה־בַּיָּמִים עַד שֶׁאֵינִי יוֹדְעָהּ עוֹד.
לְהִתְרָאוֹת אֲהוּבָה, קָשֶׁה לְשַׁעֵר.

PHILOMENA FRANZ

Franz, who was born in 1922, is a Sinti storyteller, poet and educator, who lives near Cologne. She is a survivor of Auschwitz, Ravensbrück and Oranienburg. Her parents, godmother and five siblings did not survive.

WHEN I WAS A CHILD...

When I was a child,
I saw the stones as flowers –
the tears of hope were many-coloured.

Red and blue and yellow
smiling they blossomed in childhood's garden.

Around my shoulders a bright-coloured coat,
today I know it was a dream,
a dream that forced me to live.

Drunk with life today I stand here colourless
and keep my eyes open
for what really is.

My silent smile
shows the way to gardens of stone,
I see the light of too many scars.

Translated from the German by Jean-Boase-Beier

ALS ICH EIN KIND WAR...

Als ich ein Kind war,
sah ich die Steine als Blumen,
bunt waren die Tränen der Hoffnung.

Rot und blau und gelb
blühten sie lächelnd im Beete der Kindheit.

Um meine Schultern den Mantel der Farben,
weiß ich heute, dass es ein Traum war,
ein Traum, der mich zum Leben zwang.

Trunken von Leben steh ich heute farblos
und halte Ausschau
nach dem wirklichen Sein.

Mein taubes Lächeln
zeigt nur in steinige Gärten,
ich sehe den Schein zu vieler Narben.

YORGOS IOANNOU

Born in Thessaloniki in 1927, Ioannou repeatedly expressed his disbelief and sorrow about the disappearance of his Jewish neighbours in Thessaloniki in his poems and novels. He died in 1985.

THE JEWS' SUNFLOWERS

Every time our stairs creak
I wonder "Could it be them at last?"
then I go out and for hours on end
paint bright yellow sunflowers.

But tomorrow, till left forgotten
in the waiting room, I'll wait for
the train from Krakow

and late at night, when perhaps they alight
pale, gritting their teeth,
I'll quip with feigned indifference
"you took so long to write me".

Translated from the Greek by David Connolly

ΤΑ ΗΛΙΟΤΡΟΠΙΑ ΤΩΝ ΕΒΡΑΪΩΝ

Κάθε φορά που τρίζει η σκάλα μας
«λες να 'ναι αυτοί επιτέλους;» σκέφτομαι
κι ύστερα φεύγω και με τις ώρες
κατακίτρινα ζωγραφίζω ηλιοτρόπια.

Όμως αύριο, ώσπου να ξεχαστώ
στην αίθουσα αναμονής, το τραίνο
απ' την Κρακοβία θα περιμένω

κι αργά τη νύχτα, όταν ίσως κατεβούν
ωχροί, σφίγγοντας τα δόντια,
«αργήσατε τόσο να μου γράψετε»
θα κάνω δήθεν αδιάφορα.

STANISLAV SMELYANSKY

See the information on the poet preceding the poems 'Dancing Gypsy' (p. 102) and 'Guilty!' (p. 209). The poet appended a note to the following poem that reads: 'Pogost' (Old Slavonic) is a country churchyard.

ETERNAL HOLOCAUST

This meteorite –
Beyond the force of gravity.
Sacrificial victim
Still burning.

Into the rusted sky,
Onto the endless pogost –
Holocaust splashes its
Blood-stained dawn.

The caring world watches
With concern
As the ugly fire
Slouches towards my home.

Translated from the Russian by Veronika Krasnova

ВЕЧНЫЙ ХОЛОКОСТ

Выше притяжения
Твой метеорит,
Жертва всесожжения
Все еще горит.

В это небо ржавое,
В вековой погост –
Зарево кровавое
Плещет Холокост.

Смотрит мир заботливый
На него с трудом.
А огонь уродливый
Тянется в мой дом.

CHAWWA WIJNBERG

See the note for Wijnberg's poem 'On mummy's lap', p. 115.

DECEPTIVE

Deceptive is the ease
of the unspoken word
sweet green mountain
hiding the eruption
blue sky

blue sky without
a cloud
caught in caves
or maybe tamed
in cramped burrows
but always leaking
into the brawls of time

myriads of tiny drops
the word is almost audible
almost regret
truth is a threat
always present is the unsaid
the unsaid
that rips the wounds open

Translated from the Dutch by Marian de Vooght

SCHIJNBAAR

Schijnbaar is de eenvoud
van het verzwegen woord
zoete groene berg
waarin de eruptie ligt verscholen
blauwe hemel

blauwe hemel waar
geen wolk in drijft
gevangen in grotten
of misschien getemd
in nauwe holen
maar altijd lekt het
in het krakelen van de tijd

miriaden fijne druppels
het woord is bijna hoorbaar
bijna spijt
dreigend is de waarheid
altijd aanwezig is het ongezegde
het ongezegde
dat de wonden openrijt

ANGELA FRITZEN

Fritzen is a writer and journalist who was born in Bonn in 1974. She has Down's Syndrome, and wrote this poem as part of a 2016 exhibition in the Bundeskunsthalle in Bonn that told the story of people with Down's Syndrome, including their murder by the Nazis.

THE URNS...

The urns.
Turned into ash.
Sand.
The urns.
To have strength.

Translated from the German by Jean Boase-Beier

DIE URNEN...

Die Urnen.
Eingeäschert.
Sand.
Die Urnen.
Kraft zu haben.

NITSA DORI

Information about Dori precedes her poem 'If I did not believe in you', p. 194.

TELL US NO MORE TRAIN STORIES

Tell us no more train stories
and no more about the camps,
stop remembering the smoke at least
and don't talk about those in charge.
What we want is that some day
you should find rest from this evil
for a space,
that you may forget these memories:
you have passed on all your grief,
let us weep for you
with tears of love.

Translated from the Ladino by Anna Crowe

NO MOS CONTÉS MÁS DE TRENOS

No mos contés más de trenos
y no de los campos,
el humo no lo acodrés por lo menos
ni mos hablés de los capos.
Quieremos que un día
de este mal reposarás
un punto,
de estas memorias olvidarás;
ya mos pasates toda la dolor,
déjamos llorar por vos
con lágrimas de amor.

LAJSER AJCHENRAND

Born in Poland in 1911, Ajchenrand was living in France in 1939. He was imprisoned by the Vichy regime and arrested again when he fled to Switzerland in 1942. His mother and sister were murdered in the Majdanek concentration camp. Ajchenrand wrote all his poetry in Yiddish. He died in 1985 in Zurich.

... AND GOD GRANT...

… and God grant
that when our murderers
look inside themselves
they'll be seized with horror
at what they are.

Translated from the Yiddish by Jean Boase-Beier

... UN GIB GOT...

… un gib got
as wen undsere merder
weln in sich arajnkukn
sol sej onchapn a grojl
far sich alejn.

PAUL CELAN

Celan survived forced labour in Romania in the 1940s. He suffered greatly from guilt and trauma at the loss of his mother. See the note for the poem 'Aspen tree...' (p. 112). He lived in Paris from 1948 until his suicide in 1970.

WINDING SHEET

That which you wove of lightest yarn
I wear to honour stone.
When in the dark I waken
The screams, it wafts around them.

Often, when I ought to stammer,
it throws up forgotten folds,
and the me I am now forgives
the one I was once.

But the god of the rubbleheaps
strikes his dullest drum,
and just as the fold fell out
the Dark One wrinkles his brow.

Translated from the German by Jean Boase-Beier

TOTENHEMD

Was du aus Leichtem wobst,
trag ich dem Stein zu Ehren.
Wenn ich im Dunkel die Schreie
wecke, weht es sie an.

Oft, wenn ich stammeln soll,
wirft es vergessene Falten,
und der ich bin, verzeiht
dem, der ich war.

Aber der Haldengott
Rührt seine dumpfeste Trommel,
und wie die Falte fiel,
runzelt der Finstre die Stirn.

ABOUT THE EDITORS

JEAN BOASE-BEIER is a translator of German poetry and an academic writer, and is Translations Editor for Arc Publications. Her translations include collections by modern German poets Ernst Meister (2003), Rose Ausländer (2014), and Volker von Törne (2017). She is Professor Emerita of Literature and Translation at the University of East Anglia, where she founded the MA in Literary Translation in 1992 and ran it until 2015. Her academic work focuses on translation, style and poetry, and especially on the translation of Holocaust poetry. Recent publications include *Translating the Poetry of the Holocaust* (2015), and the co-edited volumes *Translating Holocaust Lives* (2017) and *The Palgrave Handbook of Literary Translation* (2018).

MARIAN DE VOOGHT is a Visiting Fellow at the University of Essex, where she taught courses in translation studies and on the literature of conflict. She further worked at the universities of East Anglia, Konstanz, Trondheim and Texas. She translates poetry, mainly from Dutch into English, and her translations include the collected poems of Maurice Gilliams (*The Bottle at Sea*, 2006) and *Song of Stars* by Guus Luijters (2018), a book-length poem about the Holocaust which received a PEN award. Her research focuses on political aspects of literature and canonization. She is also a Dutch teacher and has published on language learning and raising bilingual children.

ABOUT THE TRANSLATORS

Timothy Adès is a rhyming translator-poet whose awards include the John Dryden Prize and the TLS Premio Valle-Inclán Prize; one of his bilingual books of poems is Robert Desnos: *Surrealist, Lover, Resistant* from Arc Publications.

Rachel Tzvia Back is a poet, translator and professor of literature residing in the Galilee. Her award-winning collection *In the Illuminated Dark: Selected Poems of Tuvia Ruebner* was published by Hebrew Union College Press in 2015.

Jean Boase-Beier is a poetry translator and academic who works mainly on modern German poetry; she is Translations Editor for Arc Publications.

Richard Berengarten, author of more than 30 poetry books, won the Wingate Award for *The Blue Butterfly* (1992), a profound meditation on the Nazi massacre at Kragujevac. He is a Bye-Fellow of Downing College, Cambridge and a Fellow of the English Association and his latest book *Changing* is a poetic homage to the *I Ching*.

David Colmer has won several international prizes for his translations of Dutch literature.

David Connolly is retired professor of Translation Studies at the University of Thessaloniki. He has translated over forty books of poetry and fiction by modern Greek authors.

Anna Crowe is a Scottish poet and translator of Romance poetry, especially Catalan and Spanish, whose third poetry collection, *Not on the Side of the Gods*, is forthcoming in September 2019.

Vivian Eden holds a doctorate in translation studies from the University of Iowa.

DONALD GARDNER, a poet and translator, selected and translated two volumes of Remco Campert's poetry (*I Dreamed in the Cities at Night*, 2007) and *In Those Days* (2014); the latter was awarded the Vondel Prize for Literary Translation. His most recent collection of poetry is *Early Morning* (2017).

GEORGE GÖMÖRI is a Hungarian-born poet, translator and essayist. He has been living in England since 1956 and is Emeritus Fellow of Darwin College, Cambridge. His latest publication is a collection of Hungarian poetry, *Steep Path* (2018), translated with Clive Wilmer.

MARI GÖMÖRI left Hungary in 1956. After gaining her diploma from RADA, she spent thirty years working in television and as a concert promoter. She has edited several books with her husband George Gömöri.

JAMES HADLEY is Ussher Assistant Professor in Literary Translation at Trinity College Dublin, with interests in indirect translation, and Japanese translation theory, history, and practice.

SAM HAMILL was an American poet, editor and translator, and co-founder of the Copper Canyon Press. In 2003 he started the Poets Against the War movement in protest at the invasion of Iraq. He died in 2018.

IAN HIGGINS has translated French poetry of both world wars, most recently Albert-Paul Granier's *Les Coqs et les Vautours* (1917; translated as *Cockerels and Vultures*, 2013), and a selection of 102 poems in *French Poems of the Great War* (2016).

FRANCIS R. JONES is a poetry translator and professor of translation studies at Newcastle University, who has published 15 volumes of translated poetry and has won a number of prizes for his translations.

JAAN KAPLINSKI is an Estonian author who has written poetry mostly in Estonian and Russian. He studied linguistics and has translated from several languages into Estonian, but also from Estonian into English and Russian.

Tsipi Keller is a novelist and translator and the author of thirteen books. She is the recipient of several literary awards, including National Endowment for the Arts Translation Fellowships. She is the editor and translator of *Poets on the Edge: An Anthology of Contemporary Hebrew Poets* (2008).

Peter Ualrig Kennedy, a retired doctor and now an active poet with work published in several journals, is the lead organiser for *Poetrywivenhoe* in Essex. In his translations from Italian he gratefully acknowledges the support he has received from Giovanni Gravina and friends in Colchester.

Simon Knight is a freelancer of long standing, translator of an anthology of poems by Fabio Pusterla entitled *Days Full of Caves and Tigers* (2012), for which he won a Swiss Arts Council prize.

Veronika Krasnova was born in Moscow, and teaches Russian at the University of East Anglia. Her main interest is in theory and practice of poetry translation.

Jamie McKendrick has published seven books of poems and has translated the prose of Giorgio Bassani and the poems of Valerio Magrelli and Antonella Anedda.

Zelda Kahan Newman is the English-language translator of the Yiddish poet, Rivka Basman Ben-Haim. Formerly the head of Hebraic and Judaic Studies at Lehman College, City University of New York, Newman is a linguist who specializes in Yiddish, the language and its culture.

Tal Nitzan is an award winning Israeli poet, novelist and translator, with 7 poetry collections in Hebrew and 13 in translation.

Roman-Gabriel Olar is Assistant Professor in Political Science at Trinity College Dublin. His research focus includes the politics of authoritarian regimes.

Thomas Ország-Land was a Hungarian journalist, poet and translator who lived in Budapest and London. He died in 2018.

NELL REGAN is a Dublin based poet and non-fiction writer. She has been a Patrick and Katherine Kavanagh Fellow and writer in residence at the International Writing Programme, University of Iowa. Her translations of the Irish language poetry of Micheál Mac Liammóir are published in Poetry Ireland Review 126.

CECILIA ROSSI, originally from Buenos Aires, is a Lecturer in Literature and Translation at the University of East Anglia. Her translations include *Selected Poems of Alejandra Pizarnik* and *The Echo of my Mother* by Tamara Kamenszain. Her translation of Pizarnik's collections *The Last Innocence* and *The Lost Adventures* is forthcoming.

MARIA GRAZINA SLAVĖNAS (Ph.D.) is an educator, translator and former Associate Editor of the journal *Lituanus*. She lives in the vicinity of Chicago. She is the editor and translator of the bilingual anthology *Janina Degutytė, Poems / Poezija* (2003).

GERALD SMITH is Professor Emeritus of Russian in the University of Oxford; in retirement he is translating the poetry of Lev Loseff.

GUNTER SPIEβ was a German academic, an expert on Slavonic languages, especially Polish, and a passionate advocate for minority languages. He died in 2018.

LAIMA VINCĖ is a literary translator and poet who since 1988 has translated poetry, drama, fiction, and non-fiction from the archaic Lithuanian language into English.

BITITE VINKLERS is a translator of Latvian folklore and contemporary literature; recent translation collections include Imants Ziedonis, *Each Day Catches Fire: Poems*, and Knuts Skujenieks, *Seed in Snow: Poems*.

MARIAN DE VOOGHT has a PhD in Comparative Literature from the University of Texas at Austin and an MA in Dutch Language and Literature from the Radboud University Nijmegen.

CLIVE WILMER is an English poet who has translated many Hungarian poets in collaboration with George Gömöri. Their most recent book is *Steep Path* (2018), a collection of poems translated from Hungarian.

PHILIP WILSON is Tutor in Philosophy at the University of East Anglia, and has published these translations: *Luther's Breviary* (with John Gledhill); *The Bright Rose: Early German Verse 800-1280; The Histories of Alexander Neville* (with Ingrid Walton and Clive Wilkins-Jones); *Venice Saved* by Simone Weil (with Silvia Panizza).

COPYRIGHT HOLDERS AND PUBLISHERS

LIST OF AUTHORS

Arc Publications would like to thank the many people
who contributed to the crowd-funding campaign
to support the production and promotion of this book.
Without their generosity it could not
have been completed.

We would particularly like to thank
the following individuals:

Timothy Adès
Josep Lluís Aguiló
Liz Almond
Eloise Ruth Auld
Micah Baker
Ian Barnett
Harry R. Brown
A Burbidge
Cheran Rudhramoorthy
Ian Chung
Coral Coons
Kevin Crossley-Holland
Anna Crowe
Cody Dannar
Nick Dempsey
Mary Easby
Finbarr Farragher
Antoinette Fawcett
Manuel Forcano
Peter France
Tony Frazer
Iain Galbraith
Jonathan Geary
John T. Gilmore
Christopher Hailey & Esther da Costa Meyer

Anthony Gilbert
Alice Hiller
Angela Jarman
Douglas Jarman
Harriet Jarman
Rick Johnson
Rosemary Jones
José Jurado
John & Grace (Australia)
Peter Kennedy
David Lehmann
Kevin Maynard
Paul Manton
Leslie Modell
Peter Mortimer
Kevin Nunn
Jonas Oppenheimer
Dr A. N. Palmer (Andrew Palmer)
Alvin Pang
Peter Patel
Ian Patterson
Ursula Phillips
M. A. (Biddy) Ridley
Cecilia Rossi
Chiara Salomoni
Ros Schwartz
Volker Spieß
Ludwig Steinherr
Ben Styles
George Szirtes
Liza van der Wal
Tony Ward
Tom Wengraf